CALIFORNIA HISTORYMAKERS

CALIFORNIA HISTORYMAKERS

by

Alan A. Hynding

College of San Mateo

KENDALL/HUNT PUBLISHING COMPANY
Dubuque, Iowa

Copyright © 1976 by Kendall/Hunt Publishing Company

Library of Congress Catalog Card Number: 76—1103

ISBN 0—8403—1416—7

Printed in the United States of America

401416   02

To Danny and Mike

Contents

Preface

My purpose in compiling this work has been to provide a supplementary paperback book of readings to accompany standard California history texts. Instead of taking a topical approach, I have tried to personalize history for the student and general reader by focusing on biography, selecting some of the famous and a few of the not so famous. The selections that follow are brief so as to allow inclusion of as many figures from California's past as the limited scope of this volume allows.

I have admittedly been biased in my selection. I have stressed more recent personalities over figures from the ante bellum era. The Spanish, Mexican and Gold Rush periods have received far too much attention in earlier anthologies while the past century has received short shrift. I have also purposely chosen persons who seemed interesting to me rather than individuals who were merely significant. As a result, there are conspicuous omissions. I did not, for example, include studies of Leland Stanford, John Sutter or Earl Warren. But I did include sketches of Aimee Semple McPherson, Chris Buckley and "Black Ahab"—not because they changed the state's destiny but because they were representative of certain types of people and often reflected the values, aspirations and opportunities of their respective locales and eras. Others I included, such as Miguel Costansó and Luther Burbank, are there because they have been misunderstood, misrepresented or neglected in recent texts and anthologies. Beyond this I have not consciously set any quotas for particular races, ethnic groups or the sexes, or for the arts, business, politics, agriculture or other fields of endeavor—an impossible task in a book of such brief compass in any case.

To my knowledge, very few of the selections that follow have appeared before in any anthologies of California history. Besides trying to provide an interesting collection of short portraits, I have attempted to pick, wherever possible, more recent and scholarly studies over earlier popular accounts which too often have been tainted by excessive nostalgia and myopic perspective.

Alan Hynding
College of San Mateo

1

Ishi

By 1900 the Indians of California had been reduced in number to a few thousand pathetic human beings—most of whom lived in impoverished isolation on desolate reservations. There had probably been as many as 250,000 native peoples living in California when the Spaniards arrived in 1769. By 1900 it was assumed that all of the native cultures had been eradicated by the onslaught of Europeans. Then, in 1911, out of the hills of the northern Sierra came a last surviving stone age Indian. His name was Ishi, which means man in his native Yahi dialect. Taken into captivity at Oroville after being found near a slaughterhouse scavenging for bones, Ishi was brought to San Francisco. There he was befriended and his culture studied by anthropologist Alfred Kroeber and his colleagues from the University of California. The following impressions of Ishi are from a book written by Kroeber's widow, Theodora. As she indicates, Ishi made the very difficult transition from his own primitive world to the white man's modern, urban society with remarkable inner resourcefulness and dignity. But like most of his people, he succumbed to a "white man's disease", dying of tuberculosis in San Francisco in 1916. It has been said that Ishi was wise rather than smart. What is the difference? How would he have coped with today's world?

Ishi

Ishi was a man of middle stature, five feet eight inches tall, presumably born between 1860 and 1862, hence fifty-two to fifty-four years old in 1914. Pope could find no evidence of childhood disease, and Ishi did not remember having had any. Neither was there evidence of smallpox or chicken pox; no glandular abnormality, no scars from boils or burns or injury.

Skin—light reddish bronze which darkened with sun exposure, fine in texture. *Hair*—black and straight, worn long over the ears, tied in a single brush down the back. *Musculature*—well developed with even distribution of subcutaneous fat. *Teeth*—all present, strong, no evidence of decay or pyorrhoea. Molars much worn but in good condition. *Eyes*—set straight, lids Caucasian in contour. (Eye and lid contour in many California Indians suggests a more Mongoloid form.) *Breath*—sweet and free from foetor, an Indian trait noted also by Stephen Powers when he traveled amongst and wrote about California Indians in 1877. *Body odor*—faintly musty. (Non-acid.) *Nose*—strong and wide. *Chest*—full, normal. *Thighs and legs*—well-formed. Spring and leg action not that of one who in his youth had been a sprinter. Both habit and build made for endurance rather than speed.

A tireless walker. *Hands*—medium small. Size 8 glove. Palms soft and pliable, fingers tapered, fingernails ovaloid in outline, texture excellent. *Feet*—broad and strong, toes straight and unspoiled, longitudinal and transverse arches perfect. Skin of sole thick but not rough. Toenails round in outline, strong, and short.

Pope preached a sermon about feet to each of his classes in medical school after he had examined Ishi's feet and taken casts of them. Indian scouts, hunters, and ethnographers who have traveled and lived with Indians in forest, desert, or plains have commented on how quietly they walk, without the snapping of twigs underfoot and the disturbance of dirt or sand and pebbles which happens when white men walk. Pope observed and described how Ishi actually walked:

> He (Ishi) springs from the great toe which is wonderfully strong in its plantar flexion and abduction. His method of locomotion is that of rather short steps, each foot sliding

Theodora Kroeber, *Ishi in Two Worlds*. Originally published by the University of California Press; reprinted by permission of The Regents of the University of California.

along the ground as it touches. Neither the heel nor the ball of the foot seems to receive the jar of the step. The foot is placed in position cautiously, not slammed or jammed down. He progresses rather pigeon-toed, and approximates crossing the line of his progress each step.

Ishi had no history of venereal infection. He knew, in a vague and general way, that there were such diseases. He was free from sex perversion of any sort. Kroeber found that Ishi was reticent about any discussion of sex, blushing furiously if the subject came up. He did not question him about his personal sex life at all. Pope did, using a doctor's opportunity and privilege. Ishi had had very little if any actual experience in sex function; perhaps a little when he was barely pubescent. There were no women left in the tiny band whom he could have married or with whom he might have had a passing relation by the time he was grown. There was only one young woman, and she was a sister or a cousin. In any case, she stood in a sister relation to him. He was much attached to her in what seems to have been a brother-sister bond made closer by their own youth, and the older ages of the other three in the group. There was certainly fondness and tenderness in their feeling for one another; there is not the slightest evidence for construing sex interest or experience to have been a part of it.

Toward all white women whom he met during his museum years, Ishi was friendly but reserved. He was a guest for dinner and overnight many times in his friends' homes, and he lived with the Watermans for three months. During these visits he never initiated conversation with his hostess, her daughters, mother, mother-in-law, or any women guests. When a woman spoke to him he answered courteously but without looking directly at her. This behavior, it must not be forgotten, was correct Yana etiquette, a proper showing of respect. How much of it was something more than that—

a shyness born of sex starvation in a person who was reserved but not shy, generally speaking—it is impossible to say. Having accustomed himself to living without any sex life during his young years, there was, no doubt, little urge to change his ways in his late forties or early fifties, particularly among strangers.

Continuing old Yana custom, Ishi bathed daily, and daily he plucked out any beard hairs which had sprouted overnight, using tweezers of split wood. No one ever saw him at this operation except by coming on him while he was engaged in his toilet in private. Daily he brushed and combed his long hair. He washed it frequently, drying it by a filliping and beating, using a flat basket paddle. In the hills, he would have put grease on it. Pope offered him bay rum, as a city substitute, but he declined it. In the hills, his bath would have been a sweat bath. The Yana used a solution made by heating the leaves and nuts of the bay tree until they were reduced to a semisolid state, and rubbed this solution on the body after a sweat bath. It acted as a soporific, "like whisky-tee" said Ishi. Ishi kept in his clothes box a bar of scented soap and a can of talcum powder, "lady powder" he called it. These were gifts that he treasured but never used.

Ishi was orderly by nature probably, and by old habit, certainly. His clothes, toilet articles, tools, treasures, all his possessions, stood neatly on shelves in his small room, or were folded in exact arrangements, or were wrapped in paper and stored in drawers. He worked wherever he chose to in the museum, and his was the sort of work to make chips or flakes or scraps and to create disorder. But he spread newspapers or a tarpaulin to work on, cleaning everything up when he was finished. In camp, his friends found that he cleaned fish or butchered a rabbit or a deer with deftness, leaving no messy and fly-attracting scraps about, and that his cooking and dishwashing were done more quickly and neatly than their own.

This easy competence and pleasure in well-ordered arrangements of the tools and possessions of living suggests the Japanese flair for raising mere orderliness to an aesthetic of orderliness. There is a temperamental, and possibly a kinaesthetic something in this trait not to be explained by poverty in the variety of things owned, or difficulty of replacement and consequent need to take good care of them. Poverty the world over does not, *per se*, make for orderliness or aesthetic satisfaction, nor for cleanliness nor pride nor even for care in handling the little one has. The aesthetic of order and arrangement would seem to be rather something inborn, deep-seated in the individual psyche. Some cultures turn this preference and capacity into an approved value: thus the Yana and the Japanese. We do not, nor do the Mohave, to name two different value systems.

Ishi enjoyed smoking, but was not a regular or confirmed smoker, going without tobacco for weeks sometimes. Tobacco was no novelty to him, the sacred pipe being a part of ritual and ceremony and prayer with his people. The no-smoking rule which held both in the museum and the hospital he regarded as reasonable: he may well have assumed that the taboo covered more esoteric hazards than those of fire. He believed tobacco to be bad for the young, not so much for reasons of health as of propriety. Amongst his acquaintances in the museum and adjoining buildings were a few who chewed tobacco. He enjoyed this pastime with the copious spitting which is part of it, but only when he was alone with one of his tobacco-chewing companions, and always out of doors. It would have seemed to Ishi a nest-fouling performance to engage in inside a house or shelter.

Ishi liked doing all kinds of things with other people. The young internes and medical students and orderlies at the hospital drew him into their games, some of which Popey knew of only afterward. None of them could match Ishi's skill in rope climbing, nor did any of them venture onto an upper window ledge of the hospital as Ishi occasionally did. Teetering there above them, laughing, and pretending to be about to accept their "dare" to jump, he clung with his bare feet to the man-made ledge as securely as he used to cling to the high ledges in Deer Creek cañon. He was not so good as the least good of his young friends at any sort of ball game, for he was not able to throw as far or with as much accuracy as they. To be good at throwing and catching, one must have learned it early in life. Although innocent of technique, Ishi made a respectable showing in informal boxing and wrestling, and he found a friendly scuffle great fun. He was expert in certain styles of swimming, using the side stroke except in rough water, where he changed to a modified breast stroke. He knew no overhand or other fancy strokes, and, unlike the Yurok Indians, he did not dive. He was accustomed to slipping into a river at water level, but he could swim underwater with great skill and for long distances. He would walk, hunt, fish, or practice archery without fatigue all day. And he was a tireless and interested partner in any sort of work at all within his range, although Pope quaintly remarks that "Ishi was indifferent to the beauty of labor as an abstract concept. He never fully exerted himself, but apparently had unlimited endurance."

Whether it was play or work, Ishi preferred company to solitude; but not in order to compete or to excel or to demonstrate his own strength or skill. The impulse to any sort of exhibitionism was totally absent in him. He might well have found in Pope's "beauty of labor," as in the white man's strenuousness and competitiveness and wish to be first, some of the seeds of the display motive which he so shunned. This reticence may have accounted also for his strong distaste for acrobatics and tumbling, whether as participant or as audience.

Ishi was normally calm and equable of disposition, never vehement nor given to bursts of anger. He showed displeasure and on occasion some excitement when an unauthorized person touched or misplaced his belongings. He was scrupulous in never touching anything which was not his, and so watchful of museum property that he reproved Popey for picking up and putting into his pocket a museum pencil. On the other hand, nothing made him happier than to be able to give something. He would give away his arrow and spear points, even a bow which had taken many patient hours to make, or anything else from his little hoard. During the camping trip he enjoyed the role of host, cooking, ladling out, and sharing his bounty from a successful day's fishing or hunting.

Ishi was religious, his mysticism as spontaneous and unstrained as his smile. He believed according to Yana formula in the making and peopling of the world by gods and demigods, and in the *taboos* laid down by these Old Ones. He also believed in a Land of the Dead where the souls of Yana live out their shadow community existence. Christian doctrine interested him, and seemed to him to be for the most part reasonable and understandable. He held to the conviction that the White God would not care to have Indians in His home, for all Loudy told him to the contrary. It may have occurred to him that the souls of white men would fit but poorly into a round dance of Yana dead. If so, he was too polite to say so.

Perhaps it was as well Loudy did not become a missionary—he left Ishi with certain misconceptions about the story and teachings of the New Testament. When Ishi saw the cinema of the Passion Play, which moved him and which he found beautiful, he assumed that Christ was the "bad man" whose crucifixion was justified.

At ease with his friends, Ishi loved to joke, to be teased amiably and to tease in return. And he loved to talk. In telling a story, if it were long or involved or of considerable affect, he would perspire with the effort, his voice rising toward a falsetto of excitement.

Needless to say, Ishi did not learn to read beyond recognition of no smoking and electric and billboard signs which were constants of San Francisco; the letters and numbers which identified the streetcars which he rode; newspaper titles; and his reading of a clock, however that was done by him. He enjoyed funny pictures, and had no difficulty in getting their "point." Perhaps funny pictures of forty years ago were more simply comic and less narrative than most of those today, less dependent upon words for communicating their meaning.

Ishi's "broken English" was much commented upon during his life at the museum—too much, perhaps. Kroeber says that none of the staff except Sapir, whose genius was for language and who knew Northern and Central Yana, pronounced Yahi as well, or used it as idiomatically, as Ishi used English; and he estimates that by 1914 Ishi commanded an English vocabulary of at least five or six hundred words. He of course understood many words which he did not himself use. Many Yana words end on a vowel sound like Italian words. The consonantal endings of English were sometimes troublesome to Ishi as they are to Italians, and he tended to naturalize them to the sound and speech pattern familiar to him as do Italians when speaking English. "How much?" for example under Italian and Yana vowel end preference may become *How mucha?*

Before giving any further approximations of Ishi's English pronunciation, it should be said that there is risk of a misconstrual of the person in such quotations—they tend to make Ishi sound quaint or childlike, whereas he was neither. A European refugee of

Ishi's age and with no previous knowledge of English will in all likelihood attain a good mastery of English usage and vocabulary after four years here. Ishi's English vocabulary by comparison remained small and his usage relatively pidgin. But it should be understood that Ishi was simultaneously confronted with unfamiliar objects, activities, meanings, and concepts, as well as with a strange language. Book, bank, and dishpan are not difficult words to learn, you may say. But what of their difficulty if your long experience had not included the concept of writing so that you did not know what were the significances of marks on the pages of a book, much less their meaning, or if you did not know what money was, or what the purpose of a dishpan?

Ishi's *Hullo,* or if the occasion was formal, *Howdado,* were cordially said and accompanied usually with a warm smile. He retained a reluctance to the use of words of farewell. His preferred phrase was a casual, *You go?* or, alternatively, *You stay. I go.* He would add a *Goodboy* when he felt it was expected of him but his heart was not in it. For whatever personal or custom-ingrained reasons, there attached to parting a significance best not accorded recognition in words.

Besides his friends, a Sioux Indian once passed judgment on Ishi. It happened in this way. Pope and Ishi were attending a Buffalo Bill Wild West Show, of which they both were fond. There were a number of Plains Indians in the show. One of them, a tall, dignified man decked out in paint and feather war bonnet, came up to Pope and Ishi. The two Indians looked at each other in silence for several moments. The Sioux then asked in perfect English "What tribe of Indian is this?" Pope answered, "Yana, from Northern California." The Sioux then gently picked up a bit of Ishi's hair, rolled it between his fingers, looked critically into his face, and said, "He is a very high grade of Indian." When he had gone, Pope asked Ishi what he thought of the Sioux. "Him's big chiep," was Ishi's enthusiastic reply.

Ishi was not given to volunteering criticism of white man's ways. But he was observant and analytic, and, when pressed, would pass a judgment somewhat as follows. He approved of the "conveniences" and variety of the white man's world—neither Ishi nor any people who have lived a life of hardship and deprivation underrate an amelioration of those severities or scope for some comforts and even some luxuries. He considered the white man to be fortunate, inventive, and very, very clever; but childlike and lacking in a desirable reserve, and in a true understanding of Nature—her mystic face; her terrible and her benign power.

Asked how he would, today, characterize Ishi, Kroeber says, "He was the most patient man I ever knew. I mean he had mastered the philosophy of patience, without trace either of self-pity, or of bitterness to dull the purity of his cheerful enduringness." His friends all testify to cheerfulness as a trait basic to Ishi's temperament—a cheerfulness which passed, given half a chance, into a gentle hilarity. His way was the way of contentment, the Middle Way, to be pursued quietly, working a little, playing a little, and surrounded by friends.

The figure of Ishi stands, part of it in the sun, varicolored and idiosyncratic and achieved; part in deep shadow, darkened by the extent of our own ignorance and by its own disadvantagements. A biography should include something at least of the nature of these shadows, the unrealized potential, the promise unfulfilled, even in that brightest year of his life, 1914. He had only one name, not the usual two or three. He had only a museum address, although it was in very truth home to him. There was no living person with whom he could, from time to time, revel in a rapid and idiomatic exchange in the childhood tongue. Affectionate and uncorrupt, he was denied the fulfillment of wife and children, or of any sex life whatsoever. Then there was the total lack of immunity to diseases of the modern world, which had been disastrous to thousands of other Indians, and which brought to Ishi illness and untimely death.

He was unique, a last man, the last man of his world, and his experience of sudden, lonely, and unmitiated change-over from the Stone Age to the Steel Age was also unique. He was, further, a living affirmation of the credo of the anthropologists that modern man—*homo sapiens*—whether contemporary American Indian or Athenian Greek of Phidias' time, is quite simply and wholly human in his biology, in his capacity to learn new skills and new ways as a changed environment exposes him to them, in his power of abstract thought, and in his moral and ethical discriminations.

With little room for choosing, Ishi made choices as courageous and enlightened as the scope of his opportunities permitted. In the Oroville jail he chose life with a strange white man, rejecting the alternative of joining subjugated members of his own race; later he chose the dignity of an earned salary and independence, rejecting government wardship; and when "civilization" bestowed upon him the gift of tuberculosis he chose to fight it according to Popey's instructions and to accept defeat with grace, his concern being to make himself as little a burden as might be to those who cared for him.

2

Miguel Costansó

California's colorful early history has left a legacy of literally hundreds of Spanish place-names that venerate the lives of countless Catholic Saints, as well as the achievements of the state's first European inhabitants. Practically everyone has heard of Father Serra and Captain Portolá. Other Spanish pioneers like Miguel Costansó have been virtually ignored. Such are the vagaries of history. Yet Costansó's outstanding contributions as chief engineer and surveyor during the initial exploration of coastal California were extremely important in shaping future Spanish policy toward the area. He not only recorded the first accurate descriptions of the California coast and San Francisco Bay while charting the course of Portolá's historic expedition of 1769, but helped General Gálvez plan the Sacred Expedition even *before* Portolá and Serra had been brought into the enterprise. For years thereafter, following his return to Mexico, Costansó helped formulate royal policy for the defense of California. In addition to all this, his extensive writings on the region qualify him as the state's first historian. Costansó seems to have been more temperate in his judgments of California than either Serra (who adored the place) or Portolá (who detested it). Born in Barcelona and rigorously trained in military science in the mother country, Costansó spent most of his adult life in Mexico, serving his king as loyally as any other military officer. Even so, his stoic temperament must at times have yielded to feelings of longing for his distant home. It is ironic, although not unusual, that a man of Costansó's stature and influence as an officer during his own lifetime should have been so quickly forgotten. On the other hand, could it be that the authors here have *overstated* his importance?

Although Miguel Costansó was probably the best educated and most able man of all the members of Alta California's founding expedition, it is ironical that today in California, practically nothing is known of this military engineer, and no material has been uncovered relating to his birth, education, and death. Though Costansó has been neglected by contemporary historians, records in Spanish and Mexican archives and libraries leave no doubt concerning this California founder's importance and stature during his lifetime.

Costansó arrived in New Spain in 1764 with the military reorganization expedition of Lieutenant General Don Juan de Villalba. Born in Barcelona in 1741, he had entered the Corps of Engineers on January 12, 1762, with the rank of *subteniente,* as *ingeniero delineador,* after having served in the Spanish Infantry along the Catalonian and Granada coasts.

From the time of his arrival at Veracruz in 1764, until May of 1767, Costansó served under General Don Antonio Ricardos and his immediate superior, Lieutenant Colonel Miguel del Corral, in mapping and charting the coast of the Gulf of Mexico. Less than a year before Costansó left Veracruz, his first post in what was to become an extremely long career in New Spain, there were seven military engineers stationed in Veracruz and at the harbor fortification San Juan de Ulúa. Four more military engineers served the interior of New Spain, and it was to the credit of Costansó that he was selected, upon his own petition, to travel to Sonora as engineer for the Elizondo expedition, sent to control rebel natives.

Costansó served under Brigadier Domingo Elizondo for about one year, charting the battle plans and taking geographical and topographical measurements utilized in later maps. Called from Sonora by Visitor General Jose de Gálvez, Costansó continued southwest and joined Gálvez in San Blas to participate in the *junta* to decide upon the "proposed voyages to San Diego and Monterey."

It is obvious from the men that Gálvez invited—Engineer Costansó, Naval Commandant Manuel Rivero Cordero, Mathematician Antonio Faveau y Quesada, and Royal Navy Pilot Vicente Vila—that no hacks were consulted. Even Captain Gaspar de Portolá and Father Fray Junípero Serra were not present to plan the occupation of Alta California. Gálvez did not inform Portolá, who at the time was governor of Sinaloa, until after the *junta*. Consequently, to overlook Gálvez's plan and ambition to occupy Upper California, and especially to ignore the plans that Costansó helped to develop for the founding of Alta California, is historical folly.

Costansó and Gálvez crossed the Sea of Cortés and landed in the rundown former Jesuit mission fields (in Baja). Costansó was dispatched to the area north of Cape San Lucas and made scale drawings and plans of the Cape, Bahía de La Paz, and Cerralvo. Gálvez dictatorially examined the missions, reorganized administrative methods, instituted other reforms and practices, and organized the four-phased Sacred Expedition to Alta California, personally selecting Fray Junípero Serra as president of the future missions despite opposition to the project by Serra's superior.

The Sacred Expedition was a dramatic success. The *San Antonio,* commanded by Juan Pérez, discoverer of Vancouver Island, arrived first on April 11, 1769. The *San Carlos,* commanded by Vicente Vila

"Miguel Costansó," by Janet Fireman and Manuel Servin in *California Historical Quarterly* (March, 1970), pp. 3-15. Used with permission of the California Historical Society.

and carrying Engineer Costansó and Lieutenant Pedro Fages, dropped anchor on April 29. The first land expedition, led by Captain Fernando Rivera y Moncada, and accompanied by diarist Fray Juan Crespi, made camp on May 14. Finally, the Portola-Serra contingent, almost duplicating Rivera y Moncada's march, arrived at San Diego on July 1 after losing thirty-two out of forty-four Jesuit civilized Indians.

San Diego was the first European settlement in California. With the primary establishment of California, Costansó's active role in the province diminishes while that of other leaders, except Portolá, increases in importance. While Fray Junípero Serra remained in San Diego to take care of the ill, Costansó accompanied Portolá in his unsuccessful attempt to locate Monterey Bay in 1769. Miguel Costansó, who would draw up plans for the Presidio and Mission of Monterey, was appointed cosmographer of the first trek. His work in 1769 consisted of marking and mapping "the ports and lands that might be discovered, and at the port of Monterey to lay out the royal presidio that was to be founded." Costansó did his work excellently. Keeping a superb account of the entire expedition which would later be published in his famous narrative on the expeditions to Alta California, Costansó was the first man to chart impressive and beautiful San Francisco Bay.

Costansó's talent and skill as a mapmaker was no accident. As a corpsman, Costansó necessarily possessed not only military knowledge, but also technical skill. When Don Jorge Próspero, Marquis of Verboom, proposed a plan to Philip V in 1710 for the organization of a Corps of Spanish Engineers, he suggested that admittance into the new corps be dependent on several qualifications. Verboom insisted that candidates for the corps already be officers in the armed forces as much for necessary military knowledge and training as for the elite stature he designed the corps to have. Further, Verboom demanded that military engineers be trained especially in technical and scientific aptitudes in the Real Academia Militar de Matemáticas, which he established in Barcelona, modeled after the one in Brussels. By a royal decree of April 11, 1711, the Corps of Engineers of Spain was established on Verboom's plan, and with him as *Ingeniero General*. A plan of 1749 called for the stationing of 110 military engineers in the Indies, but shortly after his arrival in New Spain, Costansó was one of only eleven engineers in New Spain, the area of Spanish possessions in America that always received more engineers than any other.

Costansó and his six fellow engineers who arrived in New Spain in 1764 with Villalba, formed the core of Spain's engineering delegation to New Spain. Because of the short number of engineers in the realm, and the demand for their skills, designation of a corpsman to accompany the Sacred Expedition is one more indication of the importance placed on the project by the Visitor General and the Crown. That Costansó was selected by Gálvez is indication of the confidence and esteem in which the young engineer was held.

Despite the praise showered on Costansó for his mapping of San Francisco Bay and his drawing of plans for the presidio of Monterey, his outstanding contribution to California during his stay rests in another area. Actually, it is as an historian and writer that he truly distinguished himself. His *Diario Histórico de los viages de mar, y tierra hechos al norte de la California* (Mexico, 1770), unlike the California diaries of other founders such as Junípero Serra, Juan Crespi, and Gaspar de Portolá, is not merely a boring day by day chronicle or a ghost written memoir. Costansó's *Diario* is a valid historical account that reflects modern methodology. The diary contains background information to the occupation as well as the events themselves of the Sacred Expedition. Costansó wrote with balance, he avoided bias and trivia, and differing from other diarists, mastered grammatical Castilian. In brief, he is California's first true historian. Hubert Howe Bancroft enumerated it first among works devoted exclusively to the founding of the province. Additionally, Bancroft indirectly praised the quality of Costansó's work even more when he stated that "Crespi's diary, like that of Portolá, is a long, and, except in certain parts, a monotonous description of petty happenings not worth remembering."

It would not be because of either his cartographical contributions or his historical writings that Costansó would merit recognition in California, but rather through his recommendations for populating California and his part in establishing the Villa de Branciforte, present-day Santa Cruz. Actually, Costansó's work in populating California began with the expedition's failure to find Monterey in 1769. Costansó, according to Portolá's *Diario,* along with Fages and Rivera urged the commander to search farther north for Vizcaíno's Monterey. Just what were the true roles that Costansó, Serra, and others played later in urging that San Diego be not abandoned after the first fruitless Monterey expedition returned is difficult to assess from the nature of the sources. But that Serra's role appears to have been overstressed by some historians, especially by the hack romantics, is evident. Charles E. Chapman, the authority on the founding of Alta California, propounds that the military, consisting of Portolá, Costansó, Fages and the reputedly timid Rivera, along with the overdetermined Serra, were decided to hold California. Chapman reduces the stature of Serra and raises that of the military.

Although Costansó was only one member of the *junta* and he was not the expedition's commander, because of his previous relationship with Gálvez, he wielded great influence at San Diego. Thus, his advice should have had much more effect on Por-

tolá than that of either Lieutenant Fages or Militia Captain Rivera.

After the founding of Monterey, Costansó's influence upon the development of California would have to be felt mostly from outside the province. In 1770, shortly after the planting of permanent colonization, both Costansó and Portolá sailed for Mexico. Portolá became governor of Puebla in Mexico in 1777, where he governed until 1784. Costansó began a long career in the Mexican capital, distinguishing himself as the unofficial director of civil architecture and of improvement in the enlightenment years of the later Spanish period.

Only twenty-three years old when he arrived in New Spain, Costansó spent the next half century laboring in the New World. He was a man completely dedicated to his work, as proved by the exhaustive list of his accomplishments. Many public works commissions were assigned to the talented engineer and architect. He designed a new tobacco factory, the botanical gardens, a cock-fighting arena, a house of mercy, fountains for the main plazas, and the Academy of San Carlos for the study of the fine arts where he became a professor of geometry.

Costansó participated actively in planning for the defense of the realm during the period when the Spaniards believed England to be menacing New Spain. He surveyed and reported on the damage done to the harbor fortifications at Acapulco by an earthquake in 1776. Costansó's basic plan for Acapulco survived as the primary Pacific Coast defense. Throughout his career, viceroys and other officials consulted Costansó for his advice on various projects.

In keeping with military regulations of the day, Costansó petitioned for permission to marry in 1776. The request was granted a little over a year later for the engineer to marry Doña Manuela de Aso y Otal, who was from a fine family in New Spain. In Costansó's fifty-two years in the Corps of Engineers, he lived through the administrative and organizational changes from above that set the mold for the modern Spanish engineers. He rose in the ranks. At his death on September 27, 1814, Costansó was *director subinspector* of the Corps of Engineers, one of fourteen men in the Indies holding this prestigious post.

Although Costansó's major work took place in central Mexico, he continued from the capital, to contribute to the development of California. His first such duty was almost immediately after his arrival in Mexico, when he informed the Visitor General and the Viceroy of the successful occupation of Alta California. In 1772 Costansó once more was called upon for his expert advice on California matters. Viceroy Antonio María Bucareli received a petition from Juan Bautista de Anza for permission to open a route from Sonora to Alta California, the long-cherished dream of the Jesuits. Bucareli, in his usual methodical manner, carefully consulted his advisors in the capital and requested information from any expert witness who happened to be available. Herbert E. Bolton describes the role Costansó played:

> Bucareli referred Anza's proposal to Miguel Costansó, the brilliant young engineer who had been with Portola in New California,

where he had designed presidios and drawn beautiful maps.

> Costansó replied with characteristic clearness. His views in the case summed up the whole situation. Judging from the longitudes, Costansó concluded that by air line it was a hundred and eighty leagues from Tubac to San Diego. His estimate was not far from correct. . . .

> The proposed journey Costansó considered feasible. The mountains were rough, but . . . since the Indians crossed them, Spaniards should be able to do likewise. . . .

> Of the utility of exploration Costansó had no shadow of a doubt. The new settlements planted by Portola as such were at stake. The barren Peninsula would give no aid. The Gulf was treacherous, and the land route from Loreto to San Diego long and arduous. The sea voyage from San Blas was difficult, and the vessels too small to carry the families of the colonists. As a consequence the New California soldiers were condemned to "perpetual and involuntary celibacy . . ."

Fortuitously for Anza's name and California's future, the plan was adopted, and the presidio captain made two memorable treks in 1774 and 1775. Some two hundred colonists from Sonora and Sinaloa journeyed with Anza to California and founded the presidio of San Francisco in 1776.

3

The Gobernantes

For half a century (1770-1820) California was ruled by a succession of Spanish governors, hardly a one of whom is remembered today. Most of these men appear through the mist of receding time as dimly recalled military functionaries sent to the remote province to serve their king with reluctant loyalty. Was this really the case? In his well-researched article, Donald Nuttall gives us a composite profile of the "gobernantes" of Spanish Upper California. His conclusion that they were as a rule well qualified and loyal civil servants belies a popular stereotype that Spain's provincial governors were a rather inept lot of second rate men. Indeed, as a group they appear to have been at least the equal of their contemporaries in the British colonial service or the appointees sent out West from Washington to govern the U.S. territories during the 19th century. They were also an elite. All except one or two of the gobernantes were born in Spain, and thus had no native allegiance to the New World, much less to California. This fact placed them at some social distance from most other California colonists, who were either Mexicans or Indian neophytes. At the very least, however, it can be said of the gobernantes that, as they came and went, they provided able leadership under difficult circumstances in a neglected and far-flung outpost of Spain's sprawling North American empire. Do these men seem unqualified to you in any way? Would it have been possible for the Spanish authorities to have selected better leaders?

The Gobernantes of Spanish California: A Profile

For fifty-two years Spain confronted the problems of controlling and developing the isolated frontier province of Upper California, and considering the difficulties involved she met with substantial success. The years following the colonizing expedition of 1769-1770 witnessed a strengthening of her precarious hold on the region, and its material advance was gradual but steady. By the time the province was wrested from her grasp by Mexico's independence movement of 1821 its landscape was dotted with presidios, missions, and pueblos, and the Hispanic flavor which still pervades the State was deeply implanted in its soil.

Contributors to Spain's success in Upper California were numerous. Failure may well have come early had it not been for high officials such as Visitor General Jóse de Gálvez and Viceroy Antonio María Bucareli y Ursúa. The devoted work of the Franciscan father presidents, most notably Junípero Serra and Fermín Francisco de Lasuén, and the more than one hundred friars who served under them was vital. Nor can one overlook the indispensable sacrifices and service of the military.

None, however, was more essential to Spain's Upper California enterprise than the *gobernantes* who were given direct responsibility for the area's affairs. And in filling that critical office the crown chose well; the performances of the nine men who ruled the province were almost invariably respectable, and some were highly commendable.

Rather than being fortuitous, this circumstance reflected the proper selection of personnel. This being the case, one's curiosity leads him to wonder as to the kind of individual the king sought for the position; what, in other words, were the requisite professional and personal qualifications? Contemplation of the matter soon produces a possible solution: that the question might

well be answered by drawing a profile of the typical Upper California *gobernante,* the pen being guided by collective data gleaned from records of the incumbents' backgrounds and careers. The belief that such a project would provide that service prompted the present writer to undertake it, the results of which appear below.

When completed, the profile may also be utilized for purposes of a comparative study which would be both enlightening and interesting. Although local differences existed, Upper California and the other provinces of New Spain's northern frontier shared certain characteristics—the foremost being isolation and security threats from hostile Indians and foreign intruders—and it can be assumed that responsibility for dealing with such common problems would be entrusted to men with similar backgrounds and capabilities. To test the assumption one could trace a like profile of another of the frontier provinces, such as New Mexico. It is this writer's view that in most basic respects it would conform closely with that which follows.

Upper California's *gobernante* was invariably a military officer. That this was true simply evidences the fact a professional soldier was necessary to guide the affairs of a province which was chronically faced with the threat of attack from within or without.

Upper California's ruler was almost as certainly a *peninsular*—a full-blooded Spaniard born in Spain—for his office, as were virtually all political positions in the Spanish Indies, was reserved to members of that class. *Peninsulares,* in fact, governed the province for forty-eight of the fifty-two

"The Gobernantes of Spanish Upper California: A Profile," by Donald A. Nuttall in *California Historical Quarterly* (Fall, 1972), pp. 253-262. Used with permission of the California Historical Society.

years of its Spanish period. The exceptions were Fernando de Rivera y Moncada, who served as military commandant from 1774-1777, and José Darío Argüello, who upon the death of José Joaquín de Arrillaga in 1814 acted as governor *ad interim* until replaced about a year later by Pablo Vicente de Solá, another *peninsular*. Rivera y Moncada and Argüello probably were *criollos*— full-blooded Spaniards born in the New World.

Moreover, Upper California's political head was likely to be a Basque or a Catalan, for this was true with five of the incumbents. More striking is the fact that natives of those two regions controlled the province for forty-one of its fifty-two Spanish years. The Catalan portion—thirteen years—came early: Gaspar de Portolá and Pedro Fages ruled from 1769-1774, and Fages returned to govern from 1782-1791. The Basque domination came later but is more impressive. With the exception of Argüello's one year tenure, Basques held the Upper California governorship for the final twenty-nine years of the Spanish period: Arrillaga, 1792-1794 and 1800-1814; Diego de Borica, 1794-1800; and Solá, 1815-1822. Upper California's government, one might well conclude, had become the possession of a veritable Basque dynasty. The remaining six years of *peninsular rule* were shared by the kingdoms of Andalusia and Valencia, represented by Felipe de Neve, 1777-1782 and José Antonio Roméu, 1791-1792, respectively.

With but one probable exception, Upper California's *gobernantes* enjoyed noble status. Borica and Solá identified themselves as "hidalgo," while most of the others simply indicated "noble." Neve provides a problem in this respect, for he consistently wrote no more than "conocida," or "known," in the appropriate part of his service record, but in view of his rise within Spain's colonial system it is difficult to believe that he was other than highborn. If this conclusion

is correct, Rivera y Moncada remains as the sole Upper California ruler of common origin.

Upper California's *gobernante* most likely had begun his military career in Spain, for this was true of five of the men: Portolá, Neve, Fages, Borica, and Roméu. The other four had enrolled in New Spain. It is apparent, therefore, that peninsula-born Arrillaga and Solá traveled to the New World with civilian status.

Typically, he had entered the army as a young man, most probably in his early or mid-twenties. The extremes were Portolá, who began his soldiering at the precociously early age of sixteen, and Solá, who delayed until his thirty-fourth or thirty-fifth year.

His initial rank likely was that of a junior officer, for most had begun as a cadet, an alférez, or a sub-lieutenant. The exceptions were Solá, whose first commission was that of a militia captain, and Argüello and Arrillaga, who enlisted as common soldiers.

If his military career had been inaugurated in Europe, the odds favored his having come to New Spain after having served five years or less, this being the case with three of the five men: Fages, Borica, and Roméu. This experience-pattern, however, was most irregular, since Portola and Neve remained in the Old World for thirty and twenty years respectively before making the trans-Atlantic voyage.

Uniformity is restored, however, when the times of their transfers to the New World are considered. Portolá, Neve, Borica, and Roméu all came to New Spain in 1764, as members of a military reinforcement of the viceroyalty following the Seven Years' War. Fages arrived in 1767 with a Catalan Volunteer Company destined to join Colonel Domingo Elizondo's expedition against Sonora's rebellious Indians. Five of Upper California's *gobernantes*, therefore, began their American careers within a three year period.

Upper California's ruler most commonly had risen to the rank of lieutenant colonel by the time he assumed office. The exceptions were Portolá, when named commander of the colonizing expedition, Fages and Rivera y Moncada, when granted the lesser position of military commandant, and Arrillaga and Argüello, upon becoming governor *ad interim.* All were captains, save Fages, who was a lieutenant. Fages and Arrillaga, however were lieutenant colonels when named governor. With the exception of Roméu, whose premature death precluded such action, all those formally awarded the governorship were promoted to colonel while in office.

He was also likely to be in his fiftieth year at the outset of his rule, for that was the average age. Argüello's sixty years made him the eldest, while Fages, who was only forty when designated military commandant, was the youngest. The latter, however, was fifty-two when he ascended to the governorship.

The man, as the rank and age suggest, customarily brought considerable experience to his new office. The average length of military service had been twenty-six years, and that figure was exceeded in six instances. The range was from Argüello's forty-two years to Fages' eight at the time he was named military commandant. The latter's lack of experience, combined with his relative youth, may explain the difficulties he encountered during his first Upper California rule. He was, however, a twenty year veteran when appointed governor, and this was reflected in his more creditable performance in that capacity.

The background of Upper California's *gobernante* invariably included exposure to combat. Three of the men had campaigned in Europe: Portolá had been wounded in Italy during the War of the Austrian Succession and had participated in Spain's invasion of Portugal in the course of the Seven Years' War, while Neve and Fages had also taken part in the latter campaign. More commonly, however, his soldiering had been against frontier Indian adversaries: Fages had served in Elizondo's expedition, had fought Apaches in Sonora, and had commanded the force sent to chastise the Yumas after their destruction of the Spanish settlements on the Colorado River; Roméu had led the Colorado River expedition during its latter stages, and had faced rebellious natives in Durango and Sonora; Borica had campaigned against Apaches in New Mexico and other parts of the *Provincias Internas;* and Arrillaga and Argüello likewise had seen action on the northern frontier. Solá had experienced a type of combat shared by none of the others, for evidence indicates that he played a role in quelling the insurgent movement initiated in New Spain by Father Miguel Hidalgo y Costilla's "Grito de Dolores" of 1810.

Upper California's ruler also possessed administrative experience upon entering his new position. Portolá had served as governor of Lower California from 1767-1769, and Rivera y Moncada had held the same position under Jesuit supervision for a more prolonged period of time. Neve had been adjutant major of military units in Spain, sergeant major of the Provincial Cavalry Regiment of Querétaro in New Spain from 1765-1774, and administrator of the Jesuit temporalities in Zacatecas from 1767-1774. By the time he was named governor, Fages had commanded a Catalan Volunteer Company for many years and had been commandant of presidios Santa Cruz and El Pitic in Sonora. Roméu had been both an adjutant major and sergeant major in the Company of Dragoons of Spain and had been commandant of Presidio El Pitic in Sonora. Arrillaga was the lieutenant governor of the Californias when he assumed the governorship. Borica had commanded Presidio San Eleuzario in Neuva Vizcaya and had been an adjutant inspector of the

Provincias Internas from 1782-1793. Argüello had been commandant and habilitado, or supplymaster, of presidios Santa Barbara and San Francisco. And Solá had served as habilitado general of the California presidios from 1805-1807.

The *gobernante's* Upper California service generally comprised the twilight of both his career and life. Roméu, Arrillaga, and Borica died while in office, the latter while in Durango on leave of absence because of ill health. And to those who survived their tenure of office an average of only six to seven years of life remained. Most numerous were Portolá's sixteen; after his departure from California he visited Spain for two years in order to resolve some personal affairs, returned to New Spain to serve as governor of Puebla from 1777-1785, and then returned again to Spain, where he continued in the royal service until his death in 1786. Portolá is the only *peninsular gobernante* whose remains are interred in the land of his birth. Argüello's twelve to thirteen years follow closely behind; governor of Lower California from 1815-1822, he retired to the Guadalajara region where he deceased in late 1827 or early 1828. Rivera y Moncada survived four years as lieutenant governor of the Californias before falling at the hands of the Yumas in 1781. Fages' death in Mexico City came after three years as an officer without assignment. And Neve succumbed two years after leaving California, while serving as commandant general of the Provincias Internas. Only the death-date of Solá is uncertain. He left California in 1822 as the province's deputy to the Mexican congress, but knowledge of him after that date is limited to reports that he was not admitted to the legislative body and that he was released from the military in late 1825 or early 1826. The fact he had reached his mid-sixties, however, would lead one to conclude that his life had about run its course.

Considering the times, the longevity of Upper California's ruler was impressive, and would indicate that he characteristically enjoyed robust health. The average age at time of death was sixty-one. The range was from Argüello's seventy-four years to Romeu's fifty. Three died in their sixties and an equal number in their fifties. With the exception of Rivera y Moncada, they all deceased of natural causes.

The Upper California *gobernante's* death or retirement invariably terminated a military career of great length, for the average was almost thirty-nine years. Portolá's fifty-two years, closely followed by Argüello's forty-nine, head the list, while Solá's respectable thirty rest at the bottom. Six served for thirty-five years or more, and all except Solá in excess of thirty.

The above figures invite one final calculation—the proportion of the man's life contributed to the royal service—and the findings are remarkable. Collectively, Upper California's rulers devoted over sixty percent of their years to the military, and most of them approximated that average. Portolá's amazing seventy-six percent to Solá's forty-six comprise the span. Portolá, however, was rivaled by Neve, whose total was seventy-one percent.

As sketched thus far, the profile of Upper California's *gobernante* reveals much of his typical background and career, but the most critical lines are yet to be drawn. For of all the factors determining his qualifications for the office, and his degree of success therein, the most important were the personal traits he possessed—his personality, character, temperament, and basic capabilities. If, therefore, the complete man is to be recreated those vital facets of his being must be developed. The process will also provide a service which justice perhaps demands, for it should go far toward restoring to the nine men the human qualities of which the above clinical dissection has deprived them.

This portion of the task will be more difficult than that already completed, for rather than being a mere accumulation and treatment of factual data it will involve the making of value judgments, based upon what documents and other sources inform us of the individuals' actions and how they have contemporaneously and subsequently been viewed. With this precautionary thought in mind, we shall proceed, but only after first extending due apologies to those who might be misjudged.

Upper California's ruler without exception was a faithful servant of the crown, who conscientiously strived to fulfill his office's responsibilities as he conceived them. The fact that the individual performances were not all of equal quality was due to variations in other areas, not in that of devotion to duty.

Educationally, he always met at least the minimum requirements of his position, and in some cases he exceeded them. Those of *peninsular* nobility had all received the basic education which would be expected of their social class, and perhaps more. We are told, for example, that Solá had been carefully educated in the schools of Spain, and that he had a better education than any of his predecessors. The two *criollos*—Argüello and Rivera y Moncada—were also highly literate despite their more modest origins.

Assessment of his intelligence—or basic intellectual capacity—is less tenable, for that complex and multi-faceted mental characteristic must always be gingerly handled, and particularly in the cases of historical personages who are beyond direct observation and testing. It might suffice, therefore, to point out that only one of Upper California's *gobernantes* has been accused of lacking adequate mental acuity for the office. When in Lower California, both as governor under the Jesuits and as lieutenant governor of the Californias, Rivera y Moncada seems to have performed satisfactorily, but in Monterey with its greater responsibilities

and more complex problems he became an anxious, overly-cautious official whose delay in executing superior orders, erratic actions, and conflicts with associates—most notably Father Serra and Juan Bautista de Anza—brought both his excommunication from the church and removal from office. Concurring with José de Gálvez' contemporary view, Father Antonine Tibesar has attributed Rivera y Moncada's plight to a probable lack of intelligence, to which he adds possible aggravation by emotional factors. With that single possible exception, however, it is clear that Upper California's rulers possessed the intellectual competence required by their position.

Upper California's *gobernante* rarely, if ever, lacked courage. Most of the men had displayed valor during the course of their military careers, as is noted in their service records, and although circumstances in Upper California afforded few opportunities to demonstrate the trait, when these did arise the response generally was respectable. One could cite, for example, Portolá's dogged refusal to admit failure in the face of the multifarious problems which plagued the colonizing expedition of 1769-1770, or Neve's dedication to duty despite the illness he suffered throughout his administration. There were but two possible stains on the record: Rivera y Moncada's chronic preoccupation with what he considered to be an inadequate number of troops at his disposal; and Solá's precipitous retreat from Monterey to the Salinas Valley when confronted with the landing of Hippolyte Bouchard's motley band of Buenos Aires privateers in 1818. In fairness to the two men, however, it should be pointed out that Rivera y Moncada reportedly comported himself well in his fatal encounter with the Yumas, and that King Ferdinand VII, perhaps correctly concluding that Solá merely had shown proper prudence in dealing with overwhelming odds, rewarded his actions against Bouchard with promotion to colonel.

Success in most positions depends more upon personality and human relations than upon any other single factor, and this definitely was true of Upper California's highest office. Optimum exercise of its duties required proper rapport with two principal groups of associates in the province—the Franciscan father president and his fellow friars, and military subordinates, both officers and soldiers—and its absence in either case could mean difficulties, ineffectual rule, and ultimate removal. Fortunately, Upper California's *gobernante* typically receives high marks in this area, for although the men provide a study in extremes the findings are significantly skewed toward the favorable end of the scale.

Five of the men left records of exemplary behavior. Portolá remarkably retained the respect and affection of all his associates throughout the extremely trying days of the colonizing expedition. There has been, in fact, little but praise for the manner in which he conducted himself during that difficult period. Borica had an unusually warm relationship with Father President Lausén, a fellow Basque. Nourished by the governor's role in obtaining financial aid for the friar's destitute sister in Spain, it provided the basis for generally harmonious cooperation between the two men. And we are told that Borica was noted for kindness and courtesy in his intercourse with subordinates. Arrillaga's piousness and his closeness to the Franciscans probably threatened his receiving the derisive appellation *frailero,* and although he reportedly could be abrupt with his soldiers on occasions, the fact that they referred to him as "Papá Arrillaga" reveals their affection for him. Argüello's religiosity was such that Arrillaga labeled him "El Santo," and upon his departure the friars regretted the loss of one "who seemed like one of us." The statement that at Roméu's funeral "all who knew him displayed deep grief" speaks for itself.

Neve and Sola fare less well when human relations are assessed. The former impresses one as a capable but aloof officer who would gain the respect but little more from his military subordinates. And, as is well known, his relations with Father President Serra and his religious colleagues were notoriously bad. Unlike others who were removed from office under like conditions, Neve was upheld by superior officials, perhaps because, as has been suggested, he was merely acting as the agent of a crown which was determined to affirm royal authority in ecclesiastical affairs, a characteristic of the exaggerated regalism of the times. In Solá's case the coin is reversed. He obviously came from a devout family—one of his sisters was a nun and two of his brothers were priests—and this was reflected in his generally satisfactory relations with the Franciscans. He was, however, unpopular with his military subordinates; his aristocratic manner offended them, he was a strict disciplinarian, and on at least one occasion he struck a soldier who had displeased him.

The behavior of two of the men—Fages and Rivera y Moncada—was such that it brought their removal from office. Fages, however, deserves dual consideration. When military commandant, his inexperience in matters of command and his high-strung temperament combined to make of him a most irascible individual. Consequently, he has received such sobriquets as "Bluff Catalan" and "A veritable Peter the Headstrong," and his contemporaneous label of "El Oso" probably was not applied in recognition of his bear-hunting exploits of 1772 in the Cañada de los Osos. Regardless, he frequently clashed with fellow officers, alienated the troops under his command to the point of desertion, and carried on a constant conflict with Father President Serra, whose visit to Mexico City in 1773 brought his dismissal. By the time of his return as governor, however, he had matured, and although he occasionally had differences with the Franciscans and others, including his wife, he apparently was a much more congenial companion and associate. Rivera y Moncada's difficulties in dealing with others of equal status has been mentioned above, but he did have one redeeming human relationship; he was fond of his soldiers, and they reciprocated his affection.

With the exceptions of Rivera y Moncada and Fages, when serving as military commandant, Upper California's *gobernante* possessed a combination of the above treated traits which produced a competent and satisfactory administrator. Generally, however, he was of the type which is content merely to carry out orders with little or no inclination to devise. In Neve and Borica we find two notable exceptions, for both had the twin attributes of a progressive ruler—imagination and initiative. Neve authored the *Reglamento* under which Upper California was governed for most of its Spanish period, planned and founded the province's two enduring civilian pueblos of San Jose and Los Angeles, and established the first Spanish settlements on the Santa Barbara Channel. And in most of those projects he provided leadership for superior officials. Borica was the force behind Father President Lasuén's surge of five mission foundings during 1797-1798, advanced the material development of the missions by requisitioning artisans from Mexico, and promoted education for the children of the soldiers and settlers. Special mention should also be made of Roméu. His capabilities always were highly regarded by superiors, but the illness which handicapped him during his entire administration and terminated it with death after one year precluded their demonstration in Upper California. Otherwise, he too may well have ranked above the average cut of his fellow *gobernantes*.

A look at one final facet of our subjects' lives will reveal more of highly personal traits than of qualification for political governance. I make reference to their domestic status. Six of the nine men were married, the exceptions being Portolá, Arrillaga, and Solá, who apparently were contentedly wedded to the royal service. Upper California, however, enjoyed the presence of but four *gobernadoras,* for Neve failed to bring his wife from Seville to New Spain, and Rivera y Moncada's did not join him in the province. Roméu's family, of course, had a stay of short duration. Those of the others, however, were resident for more prolonged periods, and in two cases they experienced an increase in number; Argüello's nine progeny were born prior to his administration, but the Fages added a daughter and the Boricas two sons to their Monterey households. The Fages' dispute of 1785, a provincial *cause celebre,* has received much attention, but it can be hoped that the incident was merely an aberration in an ordinarily harmonious relationship. Nor is there reason to believe that the Boricas had anything but a happy and tranquil life together. One cannot but conclude, however, that the marriage of Argüello and Ignacia Moraga, a union of two of Spanish Upper California's more prominent families, represented the ultimate in the province's domesticity. The Argüellos were blessed with six sons and three daughters, who became the beneficiaries of effective rearing by capable and loving parents. One son became a priest, and several entered the military, including Luís Antonio, who was destined to become Upper California's first political head during its Mexican period. Better known is a daughter, María de la Concepción Marcela, whose ill-fated romance with the Russian Nikolai Petrovich Rezanov had been immortalized by the poignant poetic lines of Bret Harte.

The pen may now be set aside, for the profile is complete. The observer who stands close and carefully studies the numerous lines which constitute its structure will detect certain irregularities, but upon stepping back a few paces he will perceive a more homogeneous pattern. Before him will be a general image of the type of man the Spanish monarchs of the late eighteenth and early nineteenth centuries selected to govern the frontier province of Upper California. Their confidence generally was well placed, and their reward was a half century of effective stewardship of that remote portion of their vast American empire. The nine men whom the figure represents held an office which perhaps was of relatively modest importance, and most of their accomplishments would not loom large in the greater scheme of history. For them, however, there would always be the satisfaction of knowing that theirs was a job well done.

4

Mariano Vallejo

During the relatively brief era in which Mexico ruled California and a few dozen land rich rancheros controlled the beautiful coastal hills and valleys of the state, none surpassed Don Mariano Vallejo in wealth and prestige. Vallejo's huge rancho stretched from Sonoma across the North Bay of San Francisco into what is now Contra Costa County and beyond. Thousands of cattle and scores of native vaqueros and laborers toiled on his estates. Vallejo was one of many Californios who benefited immensely from the secularization of the enormous mission holdings during the 1830s. In fact, he actually served on one of the commissions appointed by the Mexican government to subdivide the mission lands. Some of those lands were to have gone to the Indians, but it was a handful of influential officials like Vallejo who got the land.

Among the squabbling factions of the rancho oligarchy, Vallejo often interposed a powerful moderating influence. Generally a man of amiable temperament according to most of his contemporaries, he was on friendly terms with Sutter, Larkin and other American settlers as well as with most of the other neighboring rancheros. As commander of Mexico's miliary forces in the San Francisco Bay Area at the outset of the Bear Flag Revolt, Vallejo was arrested and imprisoned by the hot-headed Fremont, even though Vallejo himself seems to have favored the American cause. Vallejo survived the onslaught of the American conquerors and the gold seekers, which destroyed his neighbor Sutter and most of the other rancheros. He lived on in a kind of splendid isolation at his somewhat reduced Sonoma estate, dying in 1890 at the age of 82. In these later years, Vallejo, with three generations of his family around him, became a patriarch of California, a living legend, and a link to a quieter, less complicated past.

Mariano Vallejo

Hardly "typical" of the settlers of Spanish and Mexican California was Don Mariano Guadalupe Vallejo. Like John Sutter he stood head and shoulders above most of the leaders of Arcadian California and, while he was never governor, he became one of the most powerful individuals in the entire province. And still the Yankee take-over of California was as disastrous for him as for Sutter or Vallejo's less impressive ranchero friends. What made Vallejo's case so distressing was that he had welcomed the Americans (and earned the name of "traitor" in some quarters, as a result) because he believed their rule would mean peace and order and growth instead of the directionless drifting of the Mexican period.

Vallejo and Sutter, rivals at first, became firm friends in mutual misfortune during the Bear Flag Revolt, Mexican War, and Gold Rush. Both were efficiently looted of their lands and other property by gringo squatters and shysters. Withal, Vallejo remained the most effective link between the two regimes and he accepted his disaster with more grace than the embittered Sutter. He lived out a useful life at his Sonoma estate, Lachryma Montis (Tears of the Mountain, so called for the hillside springs which watered his vines), a 280-acre remnant of his onetime feudal domain of tens of thousands of acres. Vallejo saw the urgent need of reconciliation between the two peoples; "Let the wound heal," he urged.

During his heyday, Vallejo's kindness and hospitality rivaled that of John Sutter, himself, and Reverend Walter Colton, U. S. Navy chaplain and Alcalde of Monterey, may have been thinking of him when he contrasted the native Californians with his fellow-Americans: "The shrewdness and sharpness of the Yankee . . . and the liberality of the Californian. . . . Give me the Californian!"

Whether Vallejo was, or was not, the most distinguished *Californio,* the "Noblest Roman of them all," as historian Rockwell D. Hunt used to insist, there is no challenging his importance to California in pre-Gold Rush days. He was born on July 7, 1808, in Monterey and profited more than most of his peers from the limited and haphazard education available from Alta California's

From *Humbugs & Heroes* by Richard Dillon. Copyright 1970 by Doubleday & Company. Reprinted with permission of Doubleday & Company, Inc.

few tutors. The young man was something of a protege of Governor Pablo Solá, who appreciated the benefits of education, and Vallejo's talents were also recognized by Governor Luis Argüello, who appointed the young man his private secretary. Later, Vallejo imported the best library in California, although the clergy was outraged since many of the books were taboo because of the *Index Librorum Prohibitorum.* Mariano entered military service as a cadet at the age of fifteen, and by the time he was twenty-three he was in command of the San Francisco garrison and elected to the provincial legislature (illegally, since he was a soldier). In 1834, he was elected an alternate delegate to the Mexican Congress but was never called to Mexico City.

But Vallejo saw himself as a soldier, not a politician. He rose from ensign to colonel and even to *commandante general* of all California. He led punitive expeditions against hostile Indians and in 1829 won a considerable reputation when he whipped the rebel forces of renegade mission Indian Estanislao (or Stanislaus). However, his achievement was tarnished by his callousness in allowing his Indian allies to murder some of his prisoners. He supported the home-rule rebellion of 1832 by the Californians against the governor, Manuel Victoria, imposed upon them by Mexico City, and took part in the Isaac Graham affair, in which a number of Americans (suspected of being filibusters) were exiled. Later, however, Vallejo tried to remain more aloof from the chaotic rebellions and counterrebellions which dominated politics during the Mexican regime. He preferred to play a lone hand rather than galloping off at the drop of a sombrero to reinforce Juan B. Alvarado or José Castro in one of their power plays. Similarly, he was able to stay out of the sticky Micheltorena War of 1844, in which the governor was thrown out and Sutter was defeated and humiliated. (Vallejo had to go to the extreme of disbanding

his military company—pretending that he could no longer afford to support it—but it worked.)

When Governor José Figueroa began to worry in 1833 about the presence of the Russians at Fort Ross and Bodega, he sent his most trusted officer, Vallejo, to reconnoiter the outpost of Russian Alaska and to make recommendations. The two men decided that a military post was necessary north of San Francisco Bay, as much to contain warlike Indians and potential Yankee filibusters as Russians, who seemed peaceable enough to Vallejo. Vallejo was not only named commander of the new post at Sonoma, he was given the title of Military Commandant and Director of Colonization of the Northern Frontier. In this new position, his power compared to that of Sutter and José Castro, *commandante general of* California. By stabilizing Mexico's northwesternmost frontier Vallejo played his greatest role in California history. He whipped hostile Indians, won over others with just treatment, and made a powerful ally in Chief Sem Yeto (Mighty Army) of the Suisunes. He, several times, put a stop to the enslaving of Indian children by Mexicans and Indians alike, even by Chief Solano himself, none other than Sem Yeto after he became a Christian.

When the missions were secularized in 1833, Vallejo was named administrator of the Sonoma Mission, San Francisco de Solano. He was so efficient that he was accused of feathering his nest at the expense of the Indians and the ex-mission. But he took better care of the Indians than almost any other administrator; he increased the livestock while the herds of the other missions dwindled away. Small wonder the governor paid little heed to the complaints against Vallejo, most of them made by two discredited priests, so demoralized that they should have been defrocked long before. Later, Vallejo would protect the mission lands and herds (and the Indians) from the plans of the Hijar-Padres Company to "colonize" the missions with newcomers from Mexico and elsewhere.

One reason why Vallejo cared little to meddle in governmental politics was that Governor Juan B. Alvarado, his nephew, was jealous of him and saw him as a rival. So he devoted himself to building up Sonoma and, in time, he became a sort of *cacique*, or chief, although his allegiance to Monterey was never in doubt, as was Sutter's. His domain, with his brother Salvador's, now stretched from Sonoma to Petaluma to Napa and all the way to Carquinez Strait. The Government paid no attention to his suggestions, reforms which might have delayed the American conquest. He repeatedly urged that the presidial companies not be allowed to waste away: "the only hope of salvation of the country, which needs positive and efficacious remedies before it is submerged in ruins." Unheeded, he built up his own extraofficial presidio at Sonoma, although he was forced to outfit and pay his troops from his own pocket most of the time. (In twenty-four years of military service to Mexico, Vallejo himself was apparently never paid so much as a plugged peso in salary.) At times, as when the governor wished to use his men in some ill-advised adventure, Vallejo could fall back on the fiction that they really constituted his private bodyguard. At another time he answered Alvarado's request for some of his men by saying. "My troops will always be ready to support the law, but not to abuse it."

The ambitious and ruthless John C. Frémont mistreated Vallejo just as he did Sutter, and, through the farce of the Bear Flag Revolt, captured and jailed Vallejo at New Helvetia. When Sutter protested the gross injustice of the act, Frémont threatened to hang the Swiss from his own oak tree. It took Commodore Robert Stockton himself to secure the release of Vallejo and his aides, on parole, from the little dictator, Frémont.

Belatedly, Vallejo was rewarded for his loyalty to the new government by being elected to the constitutional convention of 1849 in Monterey. There, he was largely responsible for naming the various counties of the state. He was also elected to the first State Senate, but his efforts to place the capitol in the town of Vallejo failed. After a brief itineracy, the capitol came to rest in Sacramento. When he heard of Marshall's discovery at Coloma, Vallejo wished his friend and erstwhile enemy the best: "As the water flows through Sutter's millrace, may the gold flow into Sutter's purse." Vallejo did virtually no gold mining himself. He devoted himself to his Sonoma estate, becoming a great vineyardist and vintner like his neighbor, Agoston Haraszthy, whose two sons married daughters of Vallejo. Don Mariano also helped Bancroft write his history of California. On January 18, 1890, Vallejo died, and with him passed the last important tie with the Mexican period of California's history.

5
Dame Shirley

She was the first acclaimed literary figure in the state's history and she earned that reputation in the mining camps at the height of the Gold Rush. Her pen name was Dame Shirley, her real name, Louise Amelia Smith Clappe. She was the wife of a struggling pioneer doctor whose practice in the mining camps of Rich Bar and Indian Bar on the Feather River brought his young bride into a world she could hardly have imagined when the couple sailed from New England for San Francisco in 1849. What was it like to be the only woman living in an isolated Sierra mining camp swarming with rough prospectors of every description at the peak of the gold fever? Dame Shirley recorded her experiences in 23 letters written during 1851 and 1852 to her sister in the East. That correspondence quickly found its way into the pages of the Marysville *Herald* and three years later appeared in San Francisco's leading literary magazine, the *Pioneer*. By 1855 Dame Shirley was a celebrity. Her vivid, sensitive observations of life in the gold camps are among the most moving and informative ever written on the subject. All the more so because they come from the pen of a woman. The Shirley Letters from the California mines have appeared in several collected editions. Here, Carl Wheat looks not just at the letters, but at the young woman who wrote them, her background, her adjustments to the hard life of the Mother Lode, her character and her enduring reputation. Many distinguished chroniclers of the Gold Rush followed her, including Bret Harte and Mark Twain. But none gave us descriptions of life at the diggings with such veracity, unflinching attention to detail and penetrating insight as Shirley. Her letters, which were her only important contribution to the literature of the West, represent not only priceless historical documents, but the very best in contemporary history. Apart from her talent as a writer, how important do you think her sex was in providing her with the special insights which make her letters so valuable?

Dame Shirley's letters from the Sierra diggings form a priceless contribution to our knowledge and understanding of that long-vanished era—the earliest flush days of the great gold rush.

She had come to California in 1849 with her physician husband, Dr. Fayette Clappe, and for more than a year they had lived in the roisterous metropolis of San Francisco. But the fogs and winds that swept through the Golden Gate had finally proved too much for the doctor's health, and after sticking it out through two winter seasons he had felt it imperative to head for a more healthful climate. Leaving his wife at the Bay, he took the trail for the upper Feather River, where, as rumor had it, the climate, though rigorous, was not too bad, and a physician might find use for his talents.

By the time Dr. Clappe reached the area in question, quite a rash of doctors had broken out in those diggings, but he finally located what seemed to be a likely spot at Rich Bar, a small but bustling camp deep in the great canyon of the Feather. There he opened his office—a rude canvas affair with a dirt floor and a few rough boxes for furniture—and there, as soon as a place could be found for her to stay, he brought his wife.

It was early summer. The year was 1851. Shirley had been waiting in the valley for news from her doctor husband. In fact, she had just written that last letter to the *Herald* from Plumas City when he appeared and rode with her into the mountains. Now, week by week and month by month, she was to address to her sister those twenty-three letters from the mines. The simple realism of these letters not only contrasts with Shirley's somewhat strained earlier contributions to the *Marysville Herald* but renders her letters from the diggings almost unequaled among the literary legacies of the gold rush.

Such writings do not, of course, spring lightly from an unpracticed or untrained hand, for, though these letters were written disjointedly over a period of a year and a half, they are finished and expertly constructed documents, and their writer was quite evidently no mere amateur with her pen. But what this lady's background might have been, or even where she hailed from in "the States," was not known until quite recent years, and oddly enough it was from a group of letters written *to* her that most of that background has been developed. From this little packet of letters, found lovingly tied in faded ribbon when their recipient died—full of days—threescore years after they were received, it has been possible to reconstruct much of Shirley's earlier life, and thus to throw light on the literary background of her celebrated letters from the California mines.

It was more than a decade before Shirley found herself at Rich Bar that Alexander Hill Everett, elder brother of Edward, sat down one day in a western Massachusetts stagecoach beside a young lady of Amherst some thirty years his junior. Though she was then barely turning twenty-one, her sparkling conversation apparently keenly interested the distinguished diplomat and man of affairs. An orphan from New Jersey, she had long since learned the repose and solace that may be found in books, but in a letter to her dated October 31, 1839 Everett wrote: "if you were to add to the love of reading the habit of writing you would find a new and inexhaustible source of comfort and satisfaction opening upon you."

It was good advice, and little Louise

From *The Shirley Letters,* by Dame Shirley. Introduction and Notes by Carl I. Wheat. Copyright 1949 by Alfred A. Knopf, Inc. Reprinted by permission of Alfred A. Knopf, Inc.

Amelia Knapp Smith proceeded to take it to heart.

It was the stark life of the rough mountain gold diggings, however, that brought out the genuine talent of this girl from New England. Those months in the grotesque and ephemeral community on Rich Bar constituted the one great, the one truly dramatic, experience of her life, and in her letters to her sister she rose to heights of expression that she had not reached before and that she would not in a long lifetime again equal. The letters that Alexander Everett wrote to her during those earlier years form a remarkable collection, not only from the standpoint of their author but for the reflection of their recipient's character and growing talent. But surely neither the well-known editor, essayist, and diplomat nor his youthful correspondent could have imagined that the letters she was to write, as "Shirley," from that wild canyon in the then still unknown land of California would one day be acclaimed as perhaps the most perfect mirror of the strange world which they so simply but so well described, or that these letters of his "fair Penitent" would overshadow by far the numerous products of his own prolific pen.

In her first letter from the mountains, dated September 13, 1851, she speaks of herself as "a shivering, frail, home-loving little thistle," but apparently the "barbarous soil" of the diggings agreed with her, and in the rude society of the mines she noted with a woman's careful eye all that went on about her. "I am bound, Molly," she wrote to her sister, "by my promise, to give you a *true* picture (as much as in me lies,) of mining life and its peculiar temptations, 'nothing extenuating nor setting down aught in malice.'" Other writers—many who were later to become well known for their descriptions of life in the gold region of Califoria—were at this very time attempting to picture in books and articles the strangely effervescent qualities of that life. Their ac-

counts of their various adventures offer much of interest, but for the most part theirs were not the eyes to see many small details that lend significance and give flavor to the picture of such a society. Only a woman writing to another woman would note such elements of the small but busy world about her, and when Shirley wrote of the travail of women in the camp, and of the primitive cabins and even more elemental tents in which she and her associates lived, she faithfully set down many little human events and many subtle facts that would inevitably have escaped the eyes of a man, but that serve to give the spirit of reality to her account. Never before nor ever again was she to pierce the depths or reach the heights of human emotion which pervade her simple words from the deep canyon of the Feather River. Shirley's letters were little noticed when they first appeared in the *Pioneer*. Many well-known writers were contributing articles and bits of poetry or fiction to this new "literary exponent," and theirs were the items that stirred the greatest current interest. Today, however, when copies of the ephemeral little magazine have become prized items of rare Californiana, much of their contents has lost its pristine charm, and it can now be seen that only in "the Shirley Letters" did the *Pioneer* rise much above the level of its current literary fellows.

Oddly enough, though known in whole or in part to a few enthusiasts on early California subjects, these letters remained hidden in hard-to-come-by files of the *Pioneer* for a full threescore years and ten. Then Thomas C. Russell of San Francisco brought out a small edition of the letters, and in 1933 the Grabhorn Press published them in two beautifully designed little volumes, again in a highly limited edition.

Almost every writer to whom her letters became known over the years acknowledged his debt to Dame Shirley. Bret Harte built upon them several of his best stories of the gold rush. Others likewise used them, and when Josiah Royce wrote of the first American decade in California, he termed the letters "the best account of an early mining camp that is known to me." The little New England lady painted so vivid a picture that it is small wonder her words have lived on. Rich Bar, whence the letters were written, was a short-lived mining camp on the East Branch of the North Fork of Feather River. Situated at the bottom of a deep canyon, it was one of several similar communities that sprang up along that stream in the wake of the so-called "Gold Lake" excitement, which in the summer of 1850 first brought miners in large numbers into these northern fringes of the gold region. Today the main line of the Western Pacific Railroad traverses the gorge, and Shirley's mining camp is remembered only in a small siding, on a hill near which a single house remains to recall the habitations and the struggles of the thousand or more miners who lived there and worked up and down the canyon from that point in 1851. One by one, as the gold played out along the river, the gold-seekers departed, and today nothing save the whistles of passing locomotives disturbs the quiet that surrounds this erstwhile busy settlement.

Shirley first saw Rich Bar before its earliest lush days were over. The miners were serious and industrious, and crime was still seemingly unknown. Later the era of lawlessness began to set in, as it does in all such communities, and lynch law took over. Even then most of the miners were law-abiding and strove to rid the camp of the lawless element, but dissolution was on its way when Shirley mounted her mule and rode back over the mountain and down into the valley below. So far as we know, she never returned to Rich Bar.

Once more in San Francisco, she turned to teaching and enjoyed a notable career, several of California's most beloved authors having been numbered among her scholars. Some, like Charles Warren Stoddard and Mary Viola Tingley Lawrence, remained staunch friends over the years, and when, in 1878, she left for the East in failing health, her old pupils joined in an affectionate farewell. (The doctor had gone out of her life, by divorce, in 1857.)

For some years she lived in New York with her actress niece, Genevieve Stebbins, frequently lecturing on art and literature to women's clubs and similar groups. Finally, full fifty years after the last letter had arrived from Alexander Everett, she found herself in a small home for elderly people presided over by a niece of Bret Harte, in New Jersey, the state where she was born. Nine years later, on February 11, 1906, at the venerable age of eighty-seven, Shirley went to join her "Father Confessor," whose advice and suggestions had meant so much to her over the intervening years. Beside her lay the little packet of his letters.

If in her earlier efforts Louise Amelia Smith displayed much of the artificiality so prevalent when she began to write, in the depths of the Feather River gorge most such literary flowers were forgotten, and she sought and found the fruit that renders her letters from the diggings so appetizing, so worth remembering, so worthy of republishing. "I take pains," she wrote, "to describe things exactly as I see them, hoping that thus you will obtain an idea of life in the mines *as it is.*"

Ride with her, then, over the mountain and discover the trail that leads to the busy diggings on Rich Bar.

6

William Gwin

Senator William Gwin was the most powerful political figure in California during the turbulent years between the Gold Rush and the outbreak of the Civil War. He was also a man with divided loyalties—to his anti-slavery constituents in his adopted state of California, and to his personal interests as a slaveholder in Mississippi. Gwin's plight personified a dilemma that faced thousands of Americans—especially Southern politicians—when the nation split over the slavery issue after Lincoln's election in 1860. To whom did a man like Gwin owe his paramount allegiance? As Gerald Stanley stresses in the article below, Gwin apparently had little difficulty in choosing to return to the South. Can he then be labeled a devious racist, a man willing to return to Mississippi to defend his property in human chattels after misleading so many anti-slavery Californians who had elected and re-elected him? Gwin's was a special kind of conflict of interest. Despite his Southern leanings, many historians regard him as a stabilizing influence on the state's hectic political life during the 1850s—a man with high influence in Washington who did much to secure needed federal services for California. Like his bitter rival for control of California's Democratic Party, David Broderick, Gwin was a carpetbagger who came West to redeem his declining political fortunes in a new state after his party's setbacks in 1848. Many other public men followed similar paths. In the complex person of William Gwin we see the attributes of both the self-serving opportunist and the eloquent and often effective champion of the needs of a frontier state. We also see a man whose attitudes on race, repugnant as they may seem today, were typical of many if not most Americans—North, South and West—in his own time.

Writing in 1876 in his *Memoirs,* William McKendree Gwin, Mississippi Congressman from 1840 to 1842 and California Senator from 1850 to 1861, explained that in 1849 he

> . . . immigrated to California (from Mississippi) for the express purpose of withdrawing himself and his posterity from that part of the country where slavery existed, believing, as he then did and subsequent events have proved, that the institution of slavery would be a curse to the white inhabitants where it prevailed.

As is often the case with reminiscences written late in life, this statement does not square with the facts. In 1864 Gwin himself wrote to his brother that he had migrated to California "determined not to make money, but to devote all my energies to obtaining and maintaining political power." Further, Evan J. Coleman, Gwin's son-in-law and the compiler of his papers, noted that Gwin did not withdraw from the institution of slavery when he moved from Mississippi but rather continued to own slaves in his native state all during the 1850's when he represented California in the United States Senate.

When Gwin wrote his *Memoirs,* however, he characterized himself as a moderate on slavery and secession. He said his views on those two subjects were "persistently misunderstood" and asserted that "no living man was more devoted to the Union of the States." Like Jefferson Davis, the ex-President of the Confederate States of America, Gwin toiled during Reconstruction trying to justify his support for the South's "lost cause."

Most of Gwin's contempories saw him differently. Because of his Southern background and his speeches in the Senate on the eve of the Civil War, his political foes in California called him a "pro-slavery conspirator," a "disunionist," and a "treasonable

Senator William Gwin: Moderate or Racist?

Judas." One of his admirers, Samuel Sullivan Cox, said of Gwin, "He gave his whole heart to the cause of the Confederacy."

Historians of California politics writing at the turn of the century also denied Gwin's self-proclaimed moderation. In his multivolume *History of California,* Hubert Howe Bancroft focused on one of Gwin's devisive Senate speeches and indicted him for his pro-slavery and secessionist views. Offering this same conclusion in *The Contest for California,* Elijah H. Kennedy maintained that Gwin clearly favored the preservation of slavery and urged secession in the Senate. Two other historians, James M. Guinn and Gertrude Atherton, characterized Gwin and "the chivalry" (his political machine in California) as strongly pro-slavery. The *Memoirs* notwithstanding, Gwin's contempories and these early historians were correct in their estimate of his position.

Yet more recent works dealing with Gwin and California politics during the 1850's have accepted his *Memoirs* uncritically and have concluded erroneously that he held moderate views of slavery and secession. For example, Lately Thomas, the pseudonymous author of *Between Two Empires: The Life Story of California's First Senator, William McKendree Gwin,* classified Gwin a moderate because his views on slavery were benevolent and paternalistic and because he left the South in 1849. William H. Ellison, the editor of Gwin's *Memoirs,* also believed that Gwin came to California to rid himself of slavery. Citing Gwin's vote against slavery in the California Constitutional Convention in 1849 and his paternalistic view of the institution as "authoritative evidence" of Gwin's moderation, Ellison concluded in 1940,

"Senator William Gwin: Moderate or Racist?" by Gerald Stanley in *California Historical Quarterly* (Sept. 1971), pp. 243-252. Used with permission of the California Historical Society.

In the face of Gwin's nonslavery statements and his actions from the time he arrived in California, it is difficult to understand the attacks on him as a leader of vicious southern "chivalry". . . .

Ten years later Ellison judged Gwin "a Unionist, a believer in the right of states, a loyal American citizen." More recently Donald E. Hargis accepted Ellison's argument and reaffirmed Gwin's sectional moderation.

Finally, Hallie May McPherson, whose dissertation is the most comprehensive biography of Gwin, offered this curious appraisal of his moderation:

> (As) a southern man with close family ties and property interests in the South . . . (his) sympathies were naturally with the Confederacy. On the other hand, he loved the Union and . . . he strongly advocated a policy of conciliation. . . . He believed in neither nullification nor secession, but he did believe in revolution against the violation of constitutional right.

These revisionist historians of Gwin resemble the revisionist historians of the Civil War who have stressed that many, if not most, Southerners held moderate views of slavery and were pushed into secession in 1861. Because they believe that opposing moral principles can and should be reconciled, even at the expense of human freedom, they blame "hyperemotionalism" for the war that freed black Americans. Arguing that Republicans and abolitionists hardened sectional feelings and prevented compromise, they have concluded that the Civil War was a repressible conflict. Their interpretations worship at the throne of moderation, but, more importantly, they define *immoderation* as opposition to slavery expansion rather than as opposition to slavery itself.

Nearly every historian who has written about Gwin since Gertrude Atherton's *California: An Intimate History* (1914) has failed to consider his views on slavery critically and has carefully selected parts of his public speeches on the subject to make him a moderate. Indeed, only one, Hallie May McPherson, mentioned that he still owned slaves in Mississippi in 1861.

A study of Gwin's important speeches and his voting record from 1849 to 1861, however, indicates that his desire to maintain slavery caused him personally, as an individual, to secede from the Union in 1861. While he represented California during this period, he believed slavery was the "foundation of civilization," and when he thought the institution was threatened in March, 1861, he left the Union.

Like others masquerading under the banner of states rights, Gwin believed the Union to be a Confederacy in the strict constitutional definition of the term only when it suited his purpose. Moreover, although he was a lifelong Democrat, his devotion to party fails to explain why he supported the Lecompton Constitution in 1858, Breckinridge over Douglas in 1860, and separation instead of Union in 1861. The "party loyalty" interpretation of Gwin avoids the issue that divided the Democratic party in the 1850's, and, in fact, refuses to recognize that the party was divided. Gwin's Southern view of slavery and not his devotion to states rights or party determined his ultimate political loyalty, not the reverse.

Although Thomas, Ellison, Hargis, and McPherson claimed that Gwin's vote against the establishment of slavery in California in 1849 indicated his moderation, that vote did not necessarily mean he opposed the institution. In his *Memoirs* he made plain that he felt the soil and climate of California would prohibit slavery. Besides, he came to the West for political reasons, but at the convention he discovered that the long-standing residents of California distrusted him because of his pro-slavery views. Commenting on this in his *Memoirs,* he wrote,

Their suspicions were great against members of the convention who had recently arrived in the country, and they were especially so against Mr. Gwin to whom they attributed in their imaginations the most dangerous designs upon their property in the formation of a state government.

After he voted against slavery, however, they supported him in his bid to become Senator.

The vote against slavery at Monterey was unanimous because many delegates feared that a slavery provision in the Constitution would prevent California from entering the Union. Moreover, pro-slavery and anti-slavery delegates agreed that the anti-slavery provision would serve to keep all Negroes out of the state. This united the Convention which, in fact, voted to prohibit Negroes, whether slave or free, from settling in California. Political expediency rather than moral principle explains Gwin's vote against slavery where both nature and sentiment opposed the institution already.

After California became a state, Gwin voted consistently to protect slavery elsewhere. In 1850 he opposed an attempt to abolish slavery in the District of Columbia. He voted against a repeal of the fugitive slave law in 1852, characterizing the motion as "equivalent to introducing a resolution to dissolve the Union." He also voted for the Kansas-Nebraska Act in 1854, which in its final form was more the product of the Southern slave interests than the Douglas Democrats. After Republicans and Northern Democrats interpreted the act to mean territorial legislatures could exclude slavery, however, Gwin denounced it.

When the Dred Scott decision declared slaves property and ruled that there could be no such thing as a free territory, Gwin insisted that slavery was a judicial question settled irrevocably by the Court. To Gwin blacks belonged in chains; a free Negro was a contradiction in terms. Speaking on the Dred Scott decision, Gwin declared,

If, in 1849, the decision which has been rendered in the recent Dred Scott case had been made, we should have prohibited their (free Negroes) going into California. Our people want none but the white race among us; we do not want Negroes or Chinese. . . .

After the Dred Scott decision, Gwin took bold steps to protect slavery. As chairman of the sub-committee of Democratic Senators who recommended to the Democratic caucus nominations for various committees, he wielded much power. When Stephen A. Douglas, in his famous debates with Lincoln, admitted that in spite of the Dred Scott decision territories could still prevent slavery through unfriendly legislation, Gwin had him removed as Chairman of the Committee on Territories. Then on March 23, 1858, he voted to admit Kansas as a slave state under the Lecompton Constitution, and on May 4 he supported the English Bill which would have granted public land and immediate admission of Kansas to the Union if she voted for slavery again. Finally, in the same Congress he joined the South in voting for a congressional guarantee of slavery in the territories.

In the Thirty-Sixth Congress Gwin again demonstrated his immoderation on slavery. After five Southern Senators followed their states out of the Union in January, 1861, Republicans tried to admit Kansas as a free state. Their bill passed the Senate by a vote of 36 to 16. All Republicans and all Democrats from free states voted for the bill except Senator Gwin and Milton Latham of California, who abstained. Andrew Johnson of Tennessee and John J. Crittenden of Kentucky, genuine moderates if any existed in 1861, were the only Senators from slave states to vote for the bill.

Gwin's desire to maintain slavery clearly derived from his belief that the institution was a positive good, that it was indeed necessary for the survival of white civilization. Although he refused to speak on the subject of slavery for eight years because, he said, it was "far removed from California," he articulated his position with special clarity during the first week of the Thirty-Sixth Congress.

After Senator Clement Clay of Alabama warned Northerners that the election of a Republican president in 1860 would imperil the Union, Gwin rose to agree. He charged that the non-slaveholding states were over-estimating Southern Unionism and added that the South would favor separation from the Union in the event of a Republican triumph in 1860. Arguing that secession was possible and practical, he said to the Northern Senators,

> I believe that the slaveholding States of this Confederacy can establish a separate and independent government that will be impregnable to the assaults of all foreign enemies. They have the elements of power within their own boundaries, and the elements of strength in those very institutions which are supposed in the North to be their weakness.

Then he declared that the "Northern Party" erroneously believed "that the slave hates his master, and is kept in slavery only by power and fear." On this point Gwin's position resembled George Fitzhugh's, the extreme pro-slavery Southern author who said of the Negro, "He is but a grown up child, and must be governed as a child . . . The master occupies towards him the place of parent or guardian . . ." Presenting a classic defense of slavery, Gwin said,

> Not only do they (slaves) not seek freedom, but it is a curse to them when they get it. . . . I do not believe the negro race have ever been so happy, or so nearly approached civilization, at any period from the beginning of the world to the present time, as they do in the slaveholding States of this Confederacy, in a state of slavery.

Turning to the Senate Republicans, he charged that their party "looks to the conquest of the South," and warned that "the South should be prepared for resistance." To Gwin any attempt to interfere with slav-ery constituted a challenge to biological law. He ended his speech by pleading for the preservation of the Union on these extremist terms, thereafter to remain silent on the slavery issue in the Senate.

When Gwin campaigned for John C. Breckinridge in the fall of 1860, he again proclaimed his Southern principles. In a speech in Sacrmamento on September 11, he maintained that if the nation applied Douglas's popular soverignty the Union would be jeopardized. Such a doctrine, he claimed, was "aimed directly against the equal rights of all the States in this Confederacy." After he stressed that all men who loved the Union had a "duty" to resist the doctrine of Douglas, he praised the Beckinridge platform which proclaimed the inviolate right of all citizens to take their property into territories of the United States.

Calling all those who attacked slavery "fanatics," Gwin described their demagoguery as a threat to the "foundation of civilization." Once more he characterized the South as being "able to take care of herself and to protect her rights in or out of the Union." Then he warned, "Whenever the time comes, they (Southerners) can defend their rights, even at the bayonet's point, and they will." Although Gwin said he supported Beckinridge because "he represents my views and principles," his congressional and campaign speeches, which were reprinted only in part in his defensive *Memoirs,* clearly defined the essence of those views and principles. Because of his public statements on slavery and secession, the *Daily Alta California* labeled him a "time-serving, no-principled politician" who sacrified California to the "Moloch of sectional controversy." The *San Francisco Bulletin* added that he was a "disunionist" who would eventually support a secessionist movement in the South. Time proved the *Bulletin* correct in its prediction.

Gwin's sympathy with secession and the

Southern cause manifested itself when he acted as a mediator between the Confederacy and the incoming Republican administration in March, 1861. In his negotiations he sought only to maintain peace between the two governments and not to restore the Union. When he became convinced that war was probable and slavery would be threatened, he refused to negotiate further and personally left the Union.

His peacemaking efforts at an end and his term of office having expired on March 4, Gwin left Washington on March 11 for Mississippi, his plantation, and his slaves.

He remained in Mississippi until he returned to Washington for a brief visit on April 11, 1861. At that time Attorney General Edwin M. Stanton observed that Gwin "had great confidence of the stability and power of the Confederacy" and "sympathizes strongly" with the Confederates.

Gwin then sailed to California, but by that time his political career had all but ended. In the election of 1860 the state Democratic party split into Douglas and Breckinridge factions resulting in 38,733 votes for Lincoln, 37,999 for Douglas, 33,-969 for Breckinridge and 9,111 for Bell. After the election, the new state legislature met on March 20, 1861, to elect a new Senator to fill Gwin's seat. The Republicans, who were still in a minority, joined the Douglas Democrats and elected James A. McDougall, a Democrat professing Union sentiments. Because of Gwin's known sympathy with the South, no one even mentioned his name in the balloting. Then, in the state elections of 1861, the Republicans and Douglas Democrats repudiated the right of secession and together polled more than two-thirds of the state's votes. Republicans that year elected their first governor, Leland Stanford, by a substantial plurality.

After the unionist triumph in September, 1861, Gwin cast all pretense of unionism and moderation aside and became involved in an international scheme to aid the Confederacy. A month after the election he mysteriously boarded a steamer in San Francisco for Cuba. In the Bay of Panama, he was arrested for "treasonous activities." He remained a prisoner at Fort Lafayette, New York, from November 18 to December 2, 1861, and upon his release he returned to Mississippi for nearly a year. Then he sailed to Paris where he lived until June, 1864.

While in Paris, he succeeded in interesting Napoleon III in a project to colonize the Mexican provinces of Sonora and Chihuahua, perhaps with Confederates. After conferring with the Emperor, Gwin sailed to Mexico in June, 1864, only to find that Maximilian, Napoleon's puppet on the Mexican throne, refused to give countenance to the colonization scheme. In October, 1865, after a second visit to Mexico, he returned to the South, first to Texas and then to New Orleans, where he was arrested for a second time. Although he lived for another twenty years, he had no political career after the Civil War.

Throughout the war Union generals considered Gwin a Southern conspirator. In January, 1865, General Grant warned Major General McDowell, Union commander in the Pacific, of Gwin's activities in Mexico:

> It is known that Gwin, former United States Senator from California, has gone to Mexico and taken service under the Maxmilian Government. It is understood also that he has been appointed Governor General of Sonora. The Dr. is a rebel of the most virulent order. . . . May it not be his design to entice into Sonora the dissatisfied spirits of California, and if the opportunity occurs, organize them and invade the State?

From 1849 to 1865 Gwin defended the South's peculiar institution in public speeches and in the United States Senate. His defense of the institution was economically logical, for during the period he still owned a large plantation and many slaves in Mississippi, his *Memoirs* notwithstanding.

7

William Shorey

William Shorey can hardly be considered a California history maker in the sense that he helped to alter the destiny of the state. Yet his career as a captain of several 19th century whaling ships makes him remarkable in the annals of California maritime history. As far as is known, Shorey was the first black man in California or anywhere on the Pacific Coast to achieve such a post. His achievement was all the more extraordinary, coming as it did during a time when opportunities for blacks everywhere in America were sharply limited. The strenuous duties of life at sea, however, bred a rough equality among men, who were usually judged more by merit than color. It is unlikely that Shorey could have risen to a comparable position in landbound professions like medicine or law. Shorey spent a long apprenticeship learning his difficult calling and he mastered it with consummate skill and courage. He was certainly no black Ahab, much less a half-literate Queequeg. In Shorey's time, comparatively few blacks lived in California and others were discouraged from coming here by numerous discriminatory laws against nonwhites. But unlike California's Chinese, who arrived in such large numbers that they threatened the white population's sense of security, the small number of black people who entered the state encountered little violent racial animosity. This may well account for Shorey's acceptance as a widely respected resident of the San Francisco and Oakland community in an era that saw the tragic rise of lynch law and racial segregation in the South. Still, as a black man, his opportunities, and perhaps his ambitions, were limited because of the color of his skin. We can only speculate at what more he might have achieved had he been born in a more tolerant age.

Black Ahab: William T. Shorey, Whaling Master

When one thinks of a whaling master, he usually envisions a dour and taciturn New Englander, born in some place like Provincetown, Fairhaven, or Newburyport, and sailing in the mid-nineteenth century out of Nantucket, Sag Harbor, or New Bedford. Captain William T. Shorey, however, was an ebullient and articulate Negro, a native of the British West Indies, who sailed from the Golden Gate, and who plied his fascinating trade through the first decade of the twentieth century. According to contemporary accounts he was the only black captain on the Pacific Coast—which makes his intriguing life story all the more unique.

Shorey was born on the island of Barbados in 1859. His father was a Scottish sugar planter and his mother, Rosa Frazier, described as "a beautiful creole lady," a West Indian. As the oldest of a family of eight children, it was necessary for Shorey to begin working at an early age; and when still quite young he was apprenticed to a plumber. Although slavery had been abolished on Barbados in 1834, the opportunities for a "colored man" were still limited.

Sidney Greenfield comments that the United States beckoned as the land of promise "for the many Barbadians who found little to attract them on the rigidly organized sugar island." Also the sea apparently had a strong natural attraction for Shorey, as it did for many young men reared on the island, and he shipped as a cabin boy on a vessel bound for Boston. The captain of the ship, an Englishman, "took a fancy to him" and taught him the rudiments of navigation, a subject which he continued to study avidly under the direction of Captain Whiffer D. Leach of Provincetown.

Herman Melville, the foremost chronicler of whaling, has stated that "islanders seem to make the best whalemen;" and Shorey was to prove this true. He shipped on a whaler for the first time in the mid 1870's. The whaling industry in the United States had passed its apogée two decades earlier. From humble beginnings at Easthampton and Southampton on Long Island in the mid-seventeenth century, whaling burgeoned over the ensuing decades, and

"Black Ahab: William T. Shorey, Whaling Master," by E. Berkeley Tompkins in *California Historical Quarterly* (Spring, 1972) pp. 75-83 including picture of Shorey & family. Used with permission of California Historical Society.

by the time that the United States declared its independence it was one of the nation's most important industries. Nantucket was the leading whaling port throughout the eighteenth century, and on the eve of the revolution, the little island off the Massachusetts coast had a fleet which virtually equaled that of all the other North American ports. However, New Bedford, which took up whaling seriously in 1818, rapidly surpassed Nantucket and within a few decades dominated the American whaling scene. This meant that a small New England town was the cynosure of the whaling world, for by 1850, when Melville wrote the whaling classic *Moby Dick,* "the supremacy of American whaling had been established beyond question," and U. S. ships were taking ten thousand whales annually.

The golden age of American whaling was to be relatively brief. The discovery of oil in Pennsylvania by Edwin L. Drake in 1859 marked the genesis of a vast industry whose competitive products would ultimately destroy much of whaling's *raison d'être.* The Civil War also dealt New England whaling a severe blow. The Confederate raiders *Alabama* and *Shenandoah* decimated the Northern whaling fleet, the former sinking fourteen ships, and the latter accounting for thirty-four. These depredations were to have a significant effect on William Shorey's career, for the losses were to be a factor in the shift of the bulk of the whaling industry from New England to the West Coast.

Not only war, but the ravages of nature struck the American whaling fleet at the very time when William Shorey was on the threshold of his career. In 1871 sixty-eight whaleships were lost in the Arctic ice, including twenty-two from New Bedford alone. In 1876, the year Shorey made his maiden voyage on a whaler, the Arctic again claimed a large number of ships.

In the period before the mid-nineteenth century, the whaling industry was largely monopolized by native-born Americans, "with the Yankee of the New England seaboard as the dominant type." However, by the time that Shorey became involved in whaling, only one-third of the crews were American born, a fact that probably aided him in his rapid rise through the ranks. The crews by this time were drawn from every race and more than a score of nations. This change in the ethnic and racial composition of the crews can be explained by a number of factors. During the period in the late nineteenth century when whaling was becoming a moribund trade, other facets of the national economy were booming; wages and working conditions in general were improving, while the reverse was occurring in the whaling industry.

Whaling had always been a very difficult, demanding, and dangerous occupation. Crewmen were frequently maimed or killed in pursuit of leviathan. Work on board a whaling ship was hard, unpleasant, and tedious. Living quarters were cramped and dirty. The food was tasteless and often literally rotten. Discipline was harsh. The pay was very low, and the crew had to buy necessities at exorbitant rates. Seamen frequently returned from a cruise of several years' duration with only a few dollars to their credit, and in many cases actually in debt. Given these conditions, it is little wonder that when better paying, less hazardous, and more appealing jobs became available the crews of the whaling ships became largely composed of those at the bottom of the socio-economic ladder.

E. Keble Chatterton states that the whaler's life "was likely to appeal only to three classes of men: those who had been compelled to leave the land to avoid gaol or starvation, those who thought they were going to see the world and gain adventures, and those who were determined to work their way up until they owned a whaling ship of their own." All three factors were to some degree operative in Shorey's case.

First, as a Negro in an age in which racial prejudice and discrimination were very prevalent, the number of occupations in which he might hope to find acceptance and success was somewhat limited. Also, there had always been a rough sort of democracy on board a whaler, where a man was accepted for what he could do, rather than on the color of his skin or national origin. Second, for a boy who had grown up in the sequestered confines of the island of Barbados, the chance to travel widely and see the world must have had a strong appeal. Third, Shorey did have a real determination to work his way up, and he was highly successful in this endeavor.

Shorey shipped on his first whaling voyage in 1876 from Provincetown, Massachusetts. He sailed as a "greenhand" but returned as a boat steerer—a considerably more important member of the crew. On one of his early cruises Shorey almost lost his life while pursuing a sperm whale. "Evidently enraged," he related years later, "the whale attacked first one boat, smashing it, then a second one, and then attacked the one I was in. By good fortune we were able to fire a bomb into him, which, exploding, killed him and saved us." Undaunted by such experiences, Shorey pressed on with his whaling career, "a business," Melville comments in *Omoo*, "peculiarly fitted to attract the most reckless seamen of all nations."

His rise through the ranks was a rapid one—attesting to his intelligence, skill, and determination. By 1880 he had become an officer. He sailed from Boston on November 8 as third mate on the *Emma F. Herriman,* and was promoted to first officer by the end of the voyage. The *Herriman* was a fairly typical whaler, although somewhat larger than the average at 385 tons and 118 feet in length. The cruise lasted for more than three years, which was not an unusual length of time for a whaling voyage. During this cruise, the *Herriman* traversed the North and South Atlantic, put in on the west coast of Africa, rounded the Cape of Good Hope into the Indian Ocean, and sailed on to Australia and Tasmania, through the Tasman Sea into the South Pacific and across to the west coast of South America, calling at Chile, Peru, and Panama before proceeding to San Francisco. This cruise must have been a memorable one for Shorey, not only because it was the first time he sailed as an officer, but also because it gave him his first glimpse of San Francisco, which was to be his home port for the remainder of his lengthy career.

Shorey shipped again aboard the *Herriman* in 1884 and 1885, sailing as second and then as first officer on ten-month voyages, which were typical of West Coast whaling. Then in 1886, only ten years after beginning his whaling career, he made the great step to the coveted position of command—thus becoming "the only colored captain on the Pacific Coast." This was a great tribute to Shorey's ability and stature among his fellow seamen, for the whaling captain had to be a man of many and varied talents. He had to be an experienced and skilled sailor, an excellent navigator, a shrewd trader, an intelligent and forceful leader, and able to assume all kinds of responsibility. "During the course of an average voyage," Elmo Hohman writes, the whaling master "was almost certain to act as physician, surgeon, lawyer, diplomat, financial agent, entrepreneur, taskmaster, judge (and) peacemaker. . . ." Shorey possessed all the requisite qualifications and was to prove himself one of the most able practitioners of this demanding profession.

At this stage in his life Shorey may well have resembled the swarthy "Handsome Sailor," described in the opening lines of Melville's *Billy Budd* who "with the offhand unaffectedness of natural regality . . . seemed to accept the spontaneous homage of his shipmates." He was certainly an attractive man, as numerous photographs in the possession of his daughter attest; and he was known for his charming manner. With these attributes he succeeded in winning the hand of Julia Ann Shelton, the talented daughter of one of the leading Negro families of San Francisco; and they cruised to the Hawaiian Islands in the *Herriman* on their honeymoon. The captain left his young wife in Honolulu and continued his whaling voyage to the Sea of Japan and the Okhotsk Sea, returning with a valuable cargo of 150 barrels of sperm oil, 420 barrels of whale oil, and 5000 pounds of whalebone.

In 1889, Shorey took command of the brig *Alexander.* At 136 tons and 87 feet the *Alexander* was small for a whaler, but recently built (1886) by J. W. Crowell of Cambridge, Maryland; she was a trim and graceful vessel. Shorey made two successful cruises with the *Alexander* in 1889 and 1890. Then disaster struck in 1891, and the *Alexander* was sunk in the Arctic ice pack off St. Paul's Island (part of the Pribilofs) in the Bering Sea. Shorey's skill and resourcefulness, however, managed to save the entire crew.

The owner of the *Alexander* certainly did not lose faith in Shorey, and upon his return to San Francisco immediately placed him in command of another vessel, the *Andrew Hicks.* The *Hicks* was built by J. Delano at Fairhaven, Massachusetts in 1867, and by the time Shorey took command the ship had already endured a score of years of hard service. This had taken its toll. In 1889 her captain had written to Captain David B. Adams, a part owner of the vessel: "The old *Hicks* is about the same old sixpence only getting mighty shaky; her rigging is in terrible shape about ready to fall off her. I shouldn't be surprised to see the mainmast go over the side any day. She has the same old leaks only worse than last year, twenty minutes a day steady; it's forward somewhere; you can hear it running in but can't tell where." In spite of this dismal description, and perhaps as a result of his skillful

seamanship, the *Hicks* completed eight successful voyages under Shorey's command in the decade between 1892 and 1902.

Although certainly no monomaniac, and unlike Ahab in certain other respects, Shorey pursued the whale with much of the same relentless determination. In 1894, for example, he undertook two voyages within the same year in command of different ships. He sailed on February 2, 1894 aboard the *Hicks* on a cruise to the North Pacific, which brought him back through the Golden Gate on November 6. Then after only spending less than a month ashore, he headed out on the *Gay Head,* one of the most famous of the San Francisco whalers. This voyage to the North Pacific in 1894-1895 proved to be one of the most successful of his career.

He returned, however, to the command of the *Hicks* in 1896 for six more voyages. An examination of the crew lists and shipping papers of the last three of these voyages reveals some interesting information. Writing at mid-century, Melville stated that "at the present day not one in two of the many thousand men before the mast in the American fishery are American born. . . ." Half a century later there were even fewer native-born Americans engaged in whaling, as is evidenced by Shorey's crews. Like Melville's *Pequod,* the *Hicks* had crew members from France, Portugal, Denmark, England, Ireland, China, the South Seas, and islands all over the globe. However, in addition Shorey's crews included men from Austria, Germany, Poland, Scotland, Norway, Sweden, Canada, Australia, and British Guiana. They were not only drawn from many nations, but many races as well. This is quite evident from the crew lists, but it appears even more vividly in a contemporary account, which describes the crew of the *Hicks* as "the most heterogeneous that has made port in many a day. Bright, active Americans are in the forecastle with rugged Northmen, yellow-skinned Chinese, brown

Esquimaux and kinky-haired sailors as black as ever walked the plank of a river packet." The idea of a ship's crew as a microcosm of a world society has frequently been used as a literary device, as Melville used it in *Moby Dick*; but in the case of Shorey's ships it was literally true. Like the world, the ship had its share of friction. Although the newspaper account of the 1901 voyage of the *Hicks* states that "all hands were friendly throughout the long and tedious cruise," this was not the case; and one seaman was stabbed and seriously wounded by another sailor.

At the time that Melville first sailed aboard the *Acushuet* in 1841 as a youngster of twenty-two, the majority of whaling crew members were young men like himself. Hohman states that during this period there were many ships "with crews whose average ages were little in excess of twenty years," and that it "was exceptional to find a man of thirty in a forecastle. . . ." Shorey's crews, however, were considerably older—with many men in their thirties and an average age of about 29.

After the 1902 voyage aboard the *Hicks*, Shorey took command of another vessel. The *Hicks*, however, in spite of her bedraggled condition, remained in service for another fifteen years before foundering off Cape Henry, Virginia, while in the merchant service, to which she had been transferred the year before. As Lloyd Hare comments, "one likes to think that her stout oaken heart broke because she no longer chased the whale. It is equally possible that her merchant crew was not versed in the science of coddling a decrepit whaler."

Shorey's new and final command was the whaling bark *John and Winthrop*, built at Bath, Maine, in 1876 by Goss, Sawyer, and Packard. Shorey made five voyages in the *John and Winthrop* between 1903 and 1908.

His most exciting voyage occurred in 1907. While returning from the Okhotsk Sea, the ship experienced two fierce typhoons.

Although all sails had been taken in and ship was under bare spars, second mate Joseph Manuel reported that the vessel "was driven along at a speed of fifteen knots. The ship was battened down and all hands, as far as possible, remained below. The wind and sea increased in fury, smashed the davits and carried away one of the boats, besides sweeping everything off the deck. For thirty long hours the tempest lasted, during which no one ate or slept. The man at the wheel, when the storm was at its height, was blown against the bulwarks and severely bruised and shaken." The second typhoon carried away two more boats and all the sails, and large waves swept over the decks. Were this not enough, when near the Bowsail Channel the *John and Winthrop* encountered a thick fog and when it lifted the ship was only twenty feet off a reef. The crew testified that "nothing but Captain Shorey's coolness and clever seamanship saved a wreck."

Shorey sailed on his final voyage in January of 1908. En route to the Pacific whaling grounds he put in at Honolulu, where he was very enthusiastically received. Melville comments in *Redburn* that "whalemen are far more familiar with the wonders of the deep than any other class of seamen." Certainly this was true of Captain Shorey, and he was renowned and sought after as a raconteur. A newspaper reporter who did an article on Shorey at this time stated: "He has many reminiscences to recount, and the waterfront has been reveling in whaling adventures as it might if it had suddenly taken to reading *The Cruise of the Cachelot* and other of Frank Bullen's whaling stories." Unfortunately for posterity, Shorey was content to display his whaling knowledge and eloquence orally, otherwise we might be reading today whaling chronicles by a black counterpart of Melville.

Actually Captain Shorey might have done well to turn to literature at this juncture, for whaling had become a moribund trade.

Shorey recounted that "in the old days there were as many as three hundred whalers" in the harbor at Honolulu, but by 1908 the arrival of the *John and Winthrop* was cause for special attention. The whaling bark had become an anachronism, and whaling a dying industry in the United States. Pressed by stiff competition from other products, the price of whalebone and oil steadily declined until it was no longer profitable to outfit a whaler.

Shorey retired in 1908 and spent the remaining decade of his life ashore in Oakland, California. He continued to keep his Master's license active until the year he died, perhaps still hoping to put to sea once again and to die in harness like Ahab while still in full pursuit of leviathan.

8

Collis P. Huntington

The most hated man in California during the final 30 years of the last century was undoubtedly Collis P. Huntington, the guiding force behind the state's most powerful and hated corporation, the Southern Pacific Railroad. Although not a particularly vain or arrogant man, he had a genius for antagonizing the press and the public through his rude manner and blunt opinions on matters of public policy. His railroad was out to make all the money it could through whatever means the lenient laws of the day would allow—and the public be damned! Huntington's methods included rate fixing, exorbitant freight charges to small farmers, and the bribery of public officials at all levels. Such conduct was hardly unusual in the days of the Robber Barons; Huntington was simply more open and blatant in his contempt for the public interest. Like his famous partners—Hopkins, Stanford and Crocker—Huntington had risen from humble means and come West during the Gold Rush to discover that running a store was more profitable and less hazardous than working in a mine. Unlike the other three, his energies in behalf of the railroad did not slacken once the transcontinental was completed in 1869. His early partner in the Sacramento hardware business, Mark Hopkins, was essentially a retiring bookkeeper who contributed no important leadership in the counsels of the railroad and died not long after the completion of the Central Pacific. The pompous Stanford was intoxicated by the wealth and political prominence that attended his presidency of the west's most powerful railroad. He left most of the management of the firm's growing responsibilities to Huntington, precipitating a bitter rivalry between the two men. The third partner, Charles Crocker, who had superintended construction of the Central Pacific across the Sierra, was, like Hopkins, of little value to the railroad after 1870. It is to Huntington, then, that the largest share of the credit and blame must go for the achievements and transgressions of the Southern Pacific during its long period of dominance over California's economy and political life. Corporations today seem to be much more sensitive to public opinion than in Huntington's era. Are they?

Courtesy, The Bancroft Library.

Collis Huntington

"A hard and cheery old man, with no more soul than a shark." Thus, at the end of the century, Arthur McEwen greeted Huntington's last visit to San Francisco. The phrasing of the salute is worth attention: Huntington often had the grudging respect of his enemies. An unknown epigrammatist called him "scrupulously dishonest" and added that the old man's distaste for claiming virtues he neither had nor respected made him the Coast's least convincing hypocrite. In its story of his death the San Francisco *Examiner* remarked that he had always been "ruthless as a crocodile" and went on to state that he had met death as he had met other and earlier reverses: head-on. "Had he been a soldier," wrote C. C. Goodwin, once editor of the Virginia City *Enterprise,* "he would not have depended upon tactics . . . he . . . would have struck directly at the enemy's center." Goodman likened his methods to those of Mark Hanna. The public recognized a heroic quality in the old man's ruthlessness, and journalists who set out to revile him commonly lost heart after the first few paragraphs. There was an abundance of ammunition but few vulnerable spots at which to aim. Ridicule and abuse slid off his broad, bent back as lightly as chaff. From the '60s until 1900 San Francisco's newspaper writers were as uninhibited as any in the country. Yet when they set out to flay Huntington they commonly made a bad job of it. They went through the motions, but their hearts were not in the task.

The reason is obvious. Methods of attack that had proved effective against others of the city's millionaires—and so lent spice to the game—were useless against the grim New Englander. Ridicule of his social ambitions invariably angered naive, good-natured John W. Mackay. Huntington had no social ambitions. Attack Stanford's personal popularity from any angle and at once the dailies and weeklies under his control were spurred to furious counter-attacks. Huntington was not only indifferent to popularity, it was actually distasteful to him. Thin-lipped, dandified William Sharon, in most ways as frigid as Huntington himself,

From *The Big Four,* by Oscar Lewis. Copyright 1938 by Alfred A. Knopf, Inc. Reprinted by permission of Alfred A. Knopf, Inc.

could be reached by well-aimed thrusts at his political aspirations. Huntington's letters to his red-haired confidant, Dave Colton, advertised his unyielding contempt for public offices and for those who held them. He was accused of hoarding dollars while men of less wealth were winning renown as philanthropists. He cheerfully admitted the charge. Philanthropy was no more attractive to his eyes than such kindred imbecilities as social climbing and a desire to sit in the Senate. When he astonished the West by contributing twenty-five thousand dollars to help beautify the bleak sandhills of San Francisco's new Golden Gate Park, he specified that the money be spent for an artificial waterfall. If one paid out cash and got nothing in return, logic demanded that it be spent for a useless purpose.

In a period when open-handedness was a primary obligation of every rich man, Huntington took pains to spread his reputation as a penny-squeezer. "I'll never be remembered for the money I've given away," he once told a visitor to his New York office, almost certainly with the knowledge that he was understating the case. Years later a young civil engineer in the employ of the Central Pacific wrote: "He liked to have us think he was close in money matters," then went on to record his astonishment when, after a noontime meeting in a restaurant, the miser casually paid for luncheons for five. Huntington's remark to a clerk at the Palace Hotel after he had found and corrected a twenty-five cent overcharge in his bill was repeated for decades, frequently by Huntington himself: "Young man, you can't follow me through life by the quarters I have dropped."

He once went so far as to admit: "While money-making is a good indication in a man and is evidence that he is a good man, it is not the highest quality in the world." This place was reserved for a related activity—

that of saving it. Advice to the young was in the '80s and '90s a necessary part of any interview with any rich man. Huntington's prescription followed a fixed formula: work hard and save money. He reduced success to the ultimate in simplicity; put money in the bank. The trick was not in making it but in holding on to it. One of his few public speeches was addressed, in 1891, to the youth of the village of Westchester, New York, and his two minutes of wholesome advice led inevitably to this climax: "Learn to live on a little less than you earn and thus always have a balance in the bank." Save! Don't leave a trail of quarters dropped. Nothing else was of particular importance.

In business he was cold, crafty, hard, and frequently dishonest. But there were rumors that he had a softer side. Some professed to see a trace of sentiment in the fact that he named his private cars Oneonta I and Oneonta II after the New York town where he had spent his young manhood. In his last years he sometimes grew almost poetic when he recalled certain of his early exploits in wresting dollars from the reluctant palms of his elders, and he once reproved his two-hundred-pound stepson for shooting a bird.

There is no record that he ever wanted to reform anything or, except when personal interest was involved, to change anything. He had none of the qualities of the militantly good citizen. Social and civic consciousness were meaningless phrases; a man's responsibility was to himself. He was neither a democrat nor a snob. The man who worked hard and saved his money had his respect, whatever his station. A Negro porter in his Broad Street office bought and paid for a house out of his microscopic wages, and Huntington's pleasure in the feat was spontaneous and real. In the middle '70s the ex-policeman and small-town politician Dave Colton embroidered letters to his chief with occasional references to "our class" and "us moneyed men." Huntington's replies contained no such nonsense. Whatever stood in his way he fought stubbornly and with every evidence of pleasure; everything else was immaterial, a waste of time. This attitude, often mistaken for tolerance, was merely indifference. A plan to build a local railroad north of San Francisco was brought to his attention. "Let them do what they damn please," he wrote. "But see that they keep out of our way." This attitude was maintained with admirable consistency as long as he lived. Persons who kept out of his way might do what they damn pleased. But there was one exception. The man had dignity himself and the absurdities of other rich men brought forth brief and capable bursts of profanity. Office-holders, newspaper editors and publishers, men who wanted to reform something, these were expected to be mountebanks; one could tolerate that. But a man who had made—and kept—twenty million dollars should avoid behaving like a circus clown. He shouldn't "paint himself red and climb a pole."

To the end, Huntington refrained from pole-climbing, but as he advanced into the seventies he allowed himself certain frivolities. In 1899 when he arrived for what was to prove his last visit to the Coast, reporters met his private car at Oakland Mole and accompanied the old man across the bay. Back at their offices, one reported him "as bald as the American Eagle on our dollar, and as white as one just minted"—but still as keen as a man of fifty. He was likened to Atlas, "holding up, controlling and guarding the mighty enterprise that he and his partners had created, after all his first associates had died, and he himself was an old man. . . ." There was no lack of metaphors. He was a lordly oak, towering above the forest of ordinary men. "As the first forest melted away and a new one of different species succeeded, this oak still stood; warded off all storms that were hurled against it; turned aside the damp and the frost; waved its arms in the face of the hurricane; beat back decay; healed its own wounds, sheltered its own eagles. . . ."

Not only old age, but the loss of his hair caused him annoyance. Sensitiveness over the glistening expanse of his great domed scalp was responsible for his familiar black skullcap and for the fact, often mistaken for arrogance, that his hat usually remained on his head when good manners dictated that it should be removed. On the last visit to San Francisco he was persuaded to pose for a photograph by William Keith and again the hat was not removed.

Keith's photograph of Huntington—perhaps it was preliminary to a portrait that was never painted—was several times published after its subject's death a few months later. It is that of a tired old man, stubbornly wearing his broad-brimmed hat, his trimmed mustache and short beard snow-white. The pose of his head and the expression of his eyes are characteristic; he is looking, attentive and watchful, straight ahead. His heavy shoulders are bent. Perhaps it was cold in the velvet-hung studio, for the old man had kept on not only his hat but his black overcoat, a panel of satin in its lapel catching a high light. A worn, austere figure, all black and white, against a somber background, with but one touch of frivolity: the wrinkled hand on the chair-arm has a narrow gold ring on its smallest finger.

But this Keith photograph belonged definitely to Huntington's later period, after old age had done its best to reduce him to the common level of decrepit rich men. Looking at it, much of the nonsense of his last years becomes credible; his garrulous interviews to the press, his collections of books and paintings and French furniture, his box at the Metropolitan. This tidy, benign old gentleman might have been a United States senator, or a retired grocer or clergyman living on a pension. The journalist who invented the "man of oak" simile had certainly never seen this portrait.

Another of the few photographs he permitted to reach the public is more typical. Taken some years earlier, it has no suggestion of a bulldog with its teeth drawn. Huntington there is hunched over the littered desk of his New York office, a broad, heavy, static figure, the skullcap close down to his ears. This was his normal environment, without velvet curtains: plain oak table, walls bare except for a framed photograph behind his chair, of the Newport News shipyards. The room was perhaps twelve feet square. It might have been the stationmaster's office in any village along the eleven thousand miles of railroad under his control.

The simplicity of his seventh-floor office in the Mills Building in New York reflected a lifelong dislike for elaborate settings in business—for what a later age termed "front." As far back as 1862 one of his early acts as a railroad man had been to reject a plan for an office structure for the yet unbuilt Central Pacific. He had glanced once at the drawing, then turned the sheet over, sketched a building that was described as "a slightly oversized tool-house," and stubbornly refused to approve any other. A dozen years later, when work began on the new San Francisco headquarters at Fourth and Townsend streets, appointments of the private dining-room and of the executives' offices were described as "worthy of an exclusive club." Huntington reached the Coast in time to prevent such folly and on its completion the structure was found to have all the devitalizing luxuries of a warehouse.

While he lived, the railroads under his control had no part in the business of pampering the traveling public. Rolling stock and roadbed must be kept in operating condition and it was desirable that leaks in the roofs of freight-sheds be promptly repaired. But railroad stations were utilitarian structures; he saw no point in making them look like Gothic cathedrals or Roman baths, and until after his death no Central or Southern Pacific stations bore any such resemblance. In hundreds of towns and cities of the West the original barren sheds persisted from decade to decade, their rotting boards re-covered at intervals with mustard-yellow paint of an unvarying shade, notable examples of unmitigated ugliness. "Mr. Huntington's views on architecture," wrote Willis Polk in the middle '90s, "would shame a Digger Indian."

The railroad partnership had not been in force three months before Huntington began to be referred to as the brains of the group. With this opinion he was not inclined to quarrel, but what he most admired in himself was his ability to make an investment earn a profit. Money so earned was money created; the man who built up a paying business enriched not only himself but the world. In his old age he liked to compare his methods with those of Jay Gould, picturing himself as the practical railroad man and Gould as the speculator. He once told his secretary, George Miles: "I wouldn't go into the stock market against Gould, for he would whip me at that game. That is his business. When it comes to building and operating railroads in the most efficient and economical way, I can beat him, for that is my business."

Yet beginning with Theodore Judah, dozens of his critics have stated definitely that he was not a railroad man, notwithstanding the fact that he died controlling more miles of railroad than any man before him in history. What was meant was that while railroads were good for Huntington, Huntington was not good for railroads. He entered the transportation business direct from a Sacramento hardware store, and the shopkeeper's view-point shaped all his subsequent actions. To him a railroad was merchandise in exactly the same sense as were a dozen shovels or a keg of nails. In Sacramento he and Mark Hopkins once managed to corner the supply of blasting-powder and the coup netted them thousands of dollars.

Easy money! Huntington had not been in the railroad business a week before he was planning similar exploits: a corner on the freight and passenger business between Sacramento and Nevada. Later the plan was enormously broadened. It became a scheme to control the traffic of the entire Pacific Coast. In his K Street store he had been in the habit of charging as much as he could get. What he asked for an article was determined not by what it had cost him but by how badly the customer wanted it. That was the way prices were fixed in California through the '50s; it was the way Huntington operated his railroad system as late as 1900. He was not disturbed when shouts of indignation greeted the Big Four's admission that they fixed tariffs on the basic of all the public could pay; his climb to business success had been accompanied by a series of similar shouts. He had come to regard them as a normal reaction on the part of the customer; they were a bad sign only if they were followed by a dropping off in the volume of trade. It was just a matter of striking a balance. If the buyer protested at the top of his lungs but still bought, then the merchant knew that he was making a reasonable—that is, the maximum—profit.

Born at Harwinton, Connecticut, on October 22, 1821, son of a tinker who was regarded as miserly even by his close-fisted neighbors (and who died leaving three thousand dollars in cash), Huntington needed few lessons in the arts of accumulation. In his father's household, thrift was no abstract virtue to be acquired through a reading of the pleasant axioms of Poor Richard; it was a cardinal law of existence. In rural Connecticut a century ago, cash was an extraordinarily esteemed article, to be gathered in and held at virtually any cost. At any time during Huntington's boyhood the appearance of a spendthrift in his Litchfield County countryside would have been a hardly less astonishing apparition than a live dinosaur.

In the '90s, when it had become the obligation of rich men to boast of a youth spent in poverty, the railroad magnate never had to draw on his imagination for harrowing details. Poverty, plus industry, plus thrift; this was his formula for success, and of the three, industry was not the least important. "From the time I was a child until the present I can hardly remember a time when I was not doing something." With this sentence Huntington began one of several biographical interviews, and he commonly returned to the subject every paragraph or two. What productive enterprises occupied his time until he was fourteen are not now known, but it is known that by then he had earned—and saved—over a hundred dollars. His fourteenth year (1835) was spent as "hired man" on a neighbor's farm; he received seven dollars a month and his clothes, and of course every penny was saved. With the eighty-four dollars, plus his earlier accumulations, the young Croesus—still a month short of fifteen—left New England for wider opportunities in rural New York. "From that time on," he wrote, "I have been very busy."

At Oneonta he invested his capital in a country store, in partnership with an elder brother, Solon. But he spent little time behind the counter; he had already discovered that the world is full of men eager to do routine work for low wages.

During the next dozen years one catches glimpses of the brawny, square-jawed young man pursuing the goddess of excess profits down a variety of byways: peddling jewelry to farmers' wives in Ohio and Indiana, tramping through the pre-war South on the lucrative business of collecting unpaid balances of notes bought for a few cents on the dollar; selling butter in New York City, and turning his hand to whatever else promised a quick return.

The significance of events in California subsequent to January 24, 1848 was not overlooked by the young trader. There is no evidence, however, that Huntington ever seriously intended to become a miner. In later life he looked back to the half-day he had once spent shoveling gravel from a creek-bed as one of his major mistakes in judgment. When he sailed from New York in March '49 (aged twenty-seven), he was definitely no romanticist, light-headed from the contemplation of a prospective easy fortune. He saw the gold rush merely as a more than usually promising business opportunity, and he joined the westward scramble in his usual capacity of trader. With him on the *Crescent City* went a stock of merchandise, including a number of casks of whisky, which he planned to sell—at maximum profit, of course—to the *bona fide* Argonauts.

Few adventurers who set out for the gold fields were less affected than he by the prevailing attitude of improvidence and specious optimism. Huntington foresaw the impracticability of the "mining and trading companies" then being formed everywhere in the East, and he refused to join forces with any of them. After he reached Panama, he was able to put some of these disintegrating organizations to his own use. "They quarreled," he later remarked, "and came to me. They all seemed to come to me." The quarrels commonly meant a distribution of assets— and, as the latter were usually in the form of merchandise, Huntington was able to buy stocks of desirable goods at bargain prices. Before he was on the Isthmus a week he was carrying on the most active trading of his career. He bought whatever promised to meet his two simple requirements: a quick turnover and a large profit. During his three months' enforced stay on the Isthmus—a period less industrious Argonauts spent bemoaning the lack of boats to carry them north—Huntington took a flyer in the importing business. "While I was down there, I went down to Estebula and bought a little schooner called the *Emma* and filled her up with jerked beef, potatoes, rice, sugar and syrup in great bags and brought them up to Panama and sold them." Profits averaged well above a thousand dollars a month. His buying and selling required frequent trips through the fever-laden jungle between the two coasts. Huntington estimated that he made the crossing at least twenty times. "It was only twenty-four miles," he recalled. "I walked it."

9

Chris Buckley

The career of blind Chris Buckley furnishes a case study of the rise of a representative nineteenth century big city political boss. Or was Buckley typical? Did unusual political circumstances exist in San Francisco during the 1880s to permit the rise of a blind saloon keeper to a position of unchallenged power? It is hard to imagine a political figure like Buckley attaining power of this sort today. But Buckley in many ways, like his colorful successor, Abe Ruef, a few years later, was a common—some would even say a necessary—fixture in the hectic world of American urban politics a century ago. What changes, what reforms in big city government led to the decline of men like Chris Buckley? Why are such colorful characters so rare in the political arena today? Or are they still lurking behind the scenes? Can it be said that urban government today is more efficient, less corrupt, and generally more responsive to the people than in Buckley's time?

By some uncanny metamorphosis of opinion, bad kings sometimes become good kings when they die. On April 22, 1922, a former political king of San Francisco passed away. If this man had died in 1890, instead of 1922, the newspapers would quickly have suggested that his death by acute indigestion was in some way connected to the manner by which he had gained his wealth. But in 1922, the same newspapers that had once plumbed the depths of language to find words of abuse to describe a man they found depraved and the scourge of San Francisco, now set in motion the process of myth making. The former political king passed into San Franciscans' memories not as an ex-tryant, but as an "old-timer," a "colorful" character.

This man was Christopher Augustine Buckley, whose only virtues, his political enemies declared, consisted in being named after a Christian holiday and a Christian theologian. From his saloon on Bush Street, Christopher Buckley ruled San Francisco with intelligence, efficiency, and calculated corruption. Any history of San Francisco, or indeed, of the Democratic party during the last fourth of the nineteenth century, without the story of the Blind Boss, would be as incomplete as Hamlet without the Melancholy Dane.

Time and place conspired to give Buckley an advantage in becoming a successful city boss in San Francisco. He was born in 1845 in Ireland. His family immigrated to New York, where he spent his years of youth and adolescence. In 1862, at the age of seventeen, he came to San Francisco and took a job as a horse-car conductor on the old North Beach and South Park line.

San Francisco already contained the forces that would complicate the city's growth and render it accessible to the control of a city boss. A spirit of violence and excitement, generated in the old days of the gold rush, was perpetuated by the Vigilance Committee of 1856 and through the decades of the 1870's and 1880's by the sand-lot riots, the Workingmen's party, and the antimonopoly crusades. Increasing numbers of Chinese and Catholic-Irish fanned the fire of racial, religious, and labor hatreds. The potential of great wealth and great corporations grew rapidly and sought to dominate both economic and political life. But municipal government did not keep pace. A city charter, weakened by a host of amendments, made the office of mayor an ornamental figure-piece. Civic responsibility was divided into so many parts that any centralized authority was impossible. The city grew in giant convulsions, leaving a wide gap between the ever-expanding economic organizations and the lagging agencies of government. The man who could step into this breach and act as middleman between the economic and political institutions could have the title City Boss. It required a man who had a capacity for organization and a character not overburdened by a scrupulous regard for ethics. Buckley had both in generous quantities and he spent the next twenty years searching for an opportunity to put them into practice.

By 1863 Buckley had decided that political success in San Francisco began, not behind a horse, but behind a bar. He took a job as a bartender at the Snugg Saloon, under Maguire's Opera House on Washington Street. This was the favorite rendezvous of politicians, actors, gamblers, and assorted sports about town. Twenty-six years later, a newspaper could still recall the pungent life of the Snugg Saloon as lively conversa-

By Alexander Callow, Jr. © 1956 by the Pacific Coast Branch, American Historical Association. Reprinted from *Pacific Historical Review*, Vol. 25, No. 3, pp. 261-279, by permission of the Branch.

tion, raw whisky, strong men—a place, where indeed "murder was not infrequent."

Here, Buckley met the political chieftains of the day, such men as General Hutchinson, "Billy" Carr, George Gorham, and James Gannon. More important than any of these, however, was William Higgins, with whom Buckley took an extra job as a political handy man. Higgins, a rising young Republican, was a completely incongruous figure in saloon politics. He was not only a Harvard graduate, but had trained for the church as well. His canny political sense, his repertoire of Irish blarney, his rough but genial personality, more than made up for these handicaps. In Higgins' Fifth Ward, Buckley "developed a knack for colonizing the boarding-houses and turning tricks in the rough work of the primaries." Higgins' estimation of Buckley in these days was a portent of things to come: "He's a handy man behind the ballot-box."

Buckley left San Francisco in the late sixties, wishing to strike out more on his own in business and politics. He entered partnership with a man named James Nevins to open a "groggery" in Vallejo. Soon thereafter he became secretary of the Republican County Committee of Solano. In Vallejo he "enjoyed a liberal education in Vallejo politics, then one of the best-known training schools in higher statesmanship." Part of his political training in Vallejo consisted of devising ways to capture the Navy Yard patronage, and thereby to divert the Yard's appropriations toward the prosperity of one Christopher Buckley. He was eminently successful. A newspaper estimates that "more money was expended in patching up an old hulk than now would suffice to build and equip a modern cruiser." Buckley returned to San Francisco in 1872. Judging his political opportunity, he left Vallejo a Republican and entered San Francisco a Democrat.

The Democratic party in San Francisco in the 1870's was a coterie of subbosses,

each capable of delivering a block of votes from his respective stronghold, but none deserving the title of Boss. These men were John C. Murphy, who "carried things with a high hand in the old ninth district"; Jack Mannix, a saloonkeeper, powerful on Telegraph Hill, who "preferred the logic of the hands to that of the brain"; Owen Brady, prominent on the waterfront; Al Fritz, political captain of the Gatling Gun Battery and the Nucleus Club, both extremely powerful organizations; and Sam Rainey, leader of a strong contingent from the Fire Department.

To complete his education in the seamy side of municipal politics, as well as to have an opportunity to gain prestige and power as a politician, Buckley, in partnership with Matt Fallon, opened a saloon on Bush Street. First known as a "clearing house for rogues," it was later called "Buckley's City Hall."

Only by combining the individual ward heelers into some sort of organization could Buckley ever succeed in becoming a titular boss. Therefore, he formed an alliance with Fritz, Murphy, and Rainey and helped to elect A. J. Bryant as mayor in 1875. In 1877 they were able to elect part of the city ticket. It was in these years that Buckley suffered a personal disaster: he became his own best customer. His constitution could not withstand the assault of colossal drinking bouts, and as a result he lost his eyesight. This was an affliction which could be a severe handicap to most men, but a political opponent complained that it only served to sharpen Buckley's wits.

A parallel disaster also befell the Democratic party. The magnetic and demagogic Dennis Kearney and his sand-lot riots caused thousands of Democrats to leave their organization and fill the ranks of Kearney's Workingmen's Party. From 1876 to 1879, the Democratic voting power declined from 22,000 to about 4,000. The party was demolished to the extent that "scarce a grease spot was left to mark its place." But disaster for the party spelled boon for Buckley. It gave him an opportunity to build from the wreckage of the party—now too weak to offer resistance—a tight, coherent, political engine, with Buckley as its master and the smaller bosses unified but dominated by the blind man.

By November of 1882 Buckley had achieved the full stature of city boss. Sam Rainey was his chief lieutenant, Fritz having died in 1881, and Murphy was eliminated from active duty by his fondness for the bottle. For the next eight years, with only a minor setback in 1884, Buckley held undisputed reign over the city and became one of the most powerful men in the state Democratic party. How did this blind saloon boss consolidate and maintain power? What techniques did he use to control city government? And what manner of man was this to be called "the cunningest and most corrupt politician the West ever produced to assume its leadership"?

Known as the "Caesar of the local Democracy," Buckley found that political control of San Francisco, like Gaul, was divided into three parts: first, control of the party through the County Committee; second, control of the primary elections; and third, control of the Board of Supervisors.

No primary law existed to make political parties responsible to municipal authority. The party was simply a form of private enterprise. The County Committee, for all practical purposes, was the brains and machinery of the party. By control of this committee and especially its chairman, Buckley could direct the appointment of the powerful subcommittees, like the naming of election officials. Since the number of votes returned from each polling place was limited "only by the modesty of the election officials," the importance of this latter body can be understood. The County Committee could name both date and time of the primaries; it called the convention, whose

chairman the boss could control, and the convention, in turn, would name the next County Committee. Thus a self-perpetuating machine was in order and running at the whim of the Blind Boss.

Buckley boasted that he brought the party to a higher state of perfection than any other political leader had done. In 1882 he set up his "Club Plan" which for the first time gave San Francisco a tightly organized political machine. The "Club Plan" portioned the city into forty-seven districts or clubs, each club to elect a *pro rata* number of delegates to both municipal and state convention. Each had a leader whom Buckley controlled through appointment. A masterful organizer, he also enjoyed a profound understanding of the fundamentals of human nature. He built into his clubs an *esprit de corps,* an infectious loyalty, by creating more club officers and more committee memberships than were actually needed. Thus, as many good Democrats as possible were given a sense of authority and responsibility, or as Buckley called it, "dignity." Clam bakes and "bull-head" breakfasts followed each other in dizzy succession. Circuses and personal reward in return for obedience and support was the equation upon which Buckley built his organization.

This regime was known throughout the 'eighties as "Buckley and his lambs," or in moments of acute exasperation, as "Buck's Bums." More charitable, Buckley described a typical follower as "a good fellow (who) could gather in a few simoleons without overtaxing his strength."

Like the parties which conducted them, the primary elections were run in the full spirit of *laissez faire,* regulated by no legal controls. Control of the primaries meant control of city affairs by possession of municipal offices and patronage.

In the age of the saloon boss, election day was also the occasion for a general riot and a general binge. Saloons were booming the night before and on election day liquor was practically free. Buckley's saloon was a swarming mass of eager humanity.

Control of the primaries was the least subtle of Buckley's techniques. Men were unceremoniously herded into wagons from the dives, opium dens, and the privacy of the bawdy houses—persuaded by gold, liquor, or the fist—and sent to the voting booths. Frequently they returned, in enthusiasm for the sterling character of the nominees and the promises of good government, to vote again, again, and again. A saloon boss of these lusty years recalled an election when the crews of two visiting French war ships voted. Votes were openly bought and sold. The saloons of both the Republicans and Democrats became, for a day, miniature but bullish stock markets. The fact that a man was dead was no reason why his vote could not be cast. Gimmicked ballot boxes were only an ornamental finesse because party election officials counted the votes behind locked doors where the laws of mathematics were subject to political necessity.

Election day was also a kind of masquerade party. An incredible number of moustaches suddenly appeared, only to vanish when the voter made his second trip to the voting booth to reinforce his confidence in a candidate. Ballots were thin, and, pressed together, five could easily appear as one.

The decisive factor in an election was a wild species of men—the barroom gladiators of the day, who roamed in bands on Telegraph Hill and "South of the Slot." Elections were generally determined by whether Buckley or the Republican bosses—Higgins, Kelly, and Crimmins—could offer the greatest bribe for their support. These roughnecks, or "rockrollers," many of whom had rounded off their education at Folsom or San Quentin, were known as the "push." Buckley describes them as "the boys of the bejesus order, with the spring-bottom pants, who rivaled Orpheus on the concertina, who

canted that most moving of all songs, 'Big Horse, I Love You,' in one breath and unlimbered their awful battlecry in the next."

The "push" had several useful functions: to vote, guard voting booths, stuff ballot boxes, destroy rival booths, and intimidate voters. A respectable citizen might find himself thrown into the street, "where he would meditate on the beauties of our free institutions for a few moments, and depart, a sadder if not a wiser man." As a result, voting booths were literally fortified bastilles, and the almost constant brawls and screams, and the accuracy of slingshots and brass knuckles, closely resembled, indeed, that memorable French event. Nostalgically recalling San Francisco on election day, Buckley said: "It was a rare old sight and one that attracted many students of human nature who observed the contest from afar."

Manipulation of the primaries yielded the substance that gave life to Buckley's organization—patronage. Where the "push" was the Boss's storm troopers, his municipal officers were his occupation forces. As part of the fee for Buckley's support, public servants gave the boss the patronage of their office. Judges pledged their stenographers, justices of the peace their clerks, while deputy sheriffs and assistant district attorneys were thrown in "as a matter of course." Patronage worked in a twofold manner that helped Buckley maintain his power: one, he could use municipal offices to grant favors for powerful interests, who in return gave him support; and two, these offices provided a revenue.

Thus the assessor's office could make concessions to corporations and large landowners; the coroner could favor the water company or the street railways in case of damages. And in the district attorney's office existed a harvest of political influence useful for the big and little people alike, for part of the boss's power depended on the needy, the destitute, and the bewildered immigrant.

Revenue exacted from the city offices was, in a sense, a species of blackmail. City officials were subject to assessments "based on a sliding scale—sliding to the limit that the deputy would give." The tax collector, assessor, and country clerk, for example, employed about 200 people. Their salaries ranged from $100 to $125 a month, from which Buckley received a $25 stipend each month. A large amount of this money, however, had to be invested back into the party for charities, benefits, and election payoffs.

The most important agencies for patronage were the police, fire department, judiciary, and school system. The police were not only helpful at election time to restrain the opposition, but the police judges simplified the granting of favors by leaving blank orders of discharge at the boss's saloon. All Buckley had to do was to sign the judge's name and a friend would be relieved of the embarrassment of staying in jail.

As a more compact and politically conscious unit the fire department was more important to the boss than the police. The value of Sam Rainey, a fire commissioner, as his first lieutenant is indicated by an observation of one of Buckley's contemporaries: "Any boss who had the good will of the fire department had the world politically by the tail."

Control of the Board of Supervisors, the third avenue to political rule of the city, was the source of graft that allowed Buckley to live out his old age in splendid isolation from financial worry. The supervisors, the legislative body for the city and county of San Francisco, had the power to grant franchises, fix gas and water rates, and grant contracts for municipal supplies and civic improvement. This board controlled other city offices since it was in charge of their appropriations. It could hold a recalcitrant official in check and curb any obstreperous reformer. Control of what was known as a "solid seven" of the twelve su-

pervisors gave Buckley the power to pass an ordinance; control of a "solid nine" meant the boss could override the mayor's veto. Opportunity for graft was unwittingly provided by the city charter.

The charter stated that water and gas rates were to be regulated every year. The California Electric Company and the Spring Valley Water Company, to keep their rates from being reduced and to ensure their monopoly, offered a bribe of $7,000 to $10,000 to each supervisor who complied with their wishes, and sometimes as high a fee as $25,000 for the boss to arrange the matter with his civic-minded public servants. To maintain an even more friendly relationship with the utility companies, Buckley had one device which ensured that the money the corporations spent in bribes would be returned. The fire department would campaign for better fire protection. Public pride swelled as a multitude of fire hydrants were installed—at municipal expense. Then, interestingly enough, the utility companies would lease these hydrants *to the city* for $2.50 to $5.00 per hydrant, per month. As Buckley said, "The game of politics is not a branch of the Sunday school business."

With Andrew Hallidie's experimental cable railroad up Clay Street hill, the fever for street-railroad speculation gave Buckley and his successors more lucrative graft resources. From 1880 to 1890 the supervisors were besieged with bribes to buy franchises.

As compared to the unseen, depersonalized machinery that characterizes modern city rule, the boss of the saloon age often operated quite openly. It was, in fact, the constant complaint of the reformers that even the dogs in the street knew what was going on. Buckley had his machine, but it was held together by a personal magnetism. He had to have an infinite resource of anecdotes, the ability to amuse, to deflect antagonism by tact and compromise, an uncanny judgment of men—all these to keep a crowd together night after night, until the saloon became a salon. A former politician of this age describes how a saloon boss must act:

> He must swagger into a saloon, slap down twenty dollars, call up the house and tell the bar-keeper to freeze on to the change. . . . He must never forget his lowly retainers, for whom he must find jobs, kiss their babies and send them Christmas presents. In other words it was his duty to be in close touch with all the strata of the social system. *He must not only be great but seem great.*

Buckley's first adventure in state politics came at the Democratic Convention at San Jose, in June of 1882. His newly acquired status of boss had caught the attention of George Hearst. The captialist was seeking the nomination for governor, and Buckley, who controlled a solid and powerful San Francisco delegation, was commissioned as one of Hearst's political managers. The Democratic party had regained its confidence, and the convention opened with enthusiasm.

The convention concerned itself with the one problem that was becoming unbearable to many Californians: the predatory tactics of the Central Pacific Railroad. The record of the Democratic party for the next decade was formed by the way various groups would use the antimonopoly issue toward their own political ends. While giving lip service to railroad regulation, Hearst and Buckley received the support of W. W. Stow, the political manager of the Central Pacific, and William Carr, agent for the utility corporations. To screen their tactics, Buckley showed a flair for political artistry by starting a rumor that the railroad opposed Hearst. But a newspaper argued that political artistry degenerated into political sleight-of-hand. It accused Buckley of taking the further precaution of bribing delegates. A deal was arranged with the railroad

whereby W. P. Humphreys would be backed by the Buckley delegation for Railroad Commissioner, and in return, the railroads were to furnish support for Hearst's nomination.

Buckley was to suffer from the occupational hazard of all city bosses. Sooner or later his indiscretions were to be brought to light in such an embarrassing succession that even the apathetic and cynical citizens of the Bay City found cause for indignation. In 1883 it was revealed that Fung Jing Toy, innocuously known as Little Pete, and one of the most ruthless overlords in Chinatown's history, was paying tribute to Buckley for gambling privileges. The franchise "gift" to the San Francisco Syndicate and Trust Company over the mayor's veto in 1889, did not please the public, nor did a similar giveaway the following year to the San Francisco and San Mateo Railway Company. Perhaps it was arrogance or the realization that his time was running out that made Buckley raise the fee for not reducing the water rates from $90,000 to $150,000. The Spring Valley Company refused to pay and exposed Buckley's methods by taking the case to court. It was also discovered that Buckley had used the labor of city employees to build his beautiful ranch in Livermore. What was more disstressing was the fact that he had paid them with funds out of the city treasury.

A crescendo to these events came in the elections of 1890 when Boss Buckley sold out his party to the ambitions of Leland Stanford. The deal involved an even swap. The Buckley-Hearst group was to make possible a Republican victory so that Stanford could be re-elected to the United States Senate. Stanford, in return, would provide a Democratic legislature in 1893 to re-elect "Uncle" George Hearst to the Senate. Stanford provided a fortune in bribes, and the political brokerage firm of Buckley worked with the Republican boss Higgins in buying votes and "scratching" the Democratic ticket in favor of the Stanford electors. The result was an overwhelming Republican victory in both city and state. Buckley found it expedient to take a holiday.

Scandal and an aggressive reform group, led by Gavin McNab, ended the Blind Boss's political career. With the public now highly allergic to fraud, Buckley left orders that the County Committee was to be disbanded and the municipal election of 1890 was to be fought in the manner prescribed by the reformers, on a fair and honorable basis. The rebel Democratic reformers captured control of the city organization by using not only all of Buckley's past fraudulent tactics, but by devising new ones as well. Such strategy as making a citizen reach the polling place by climbing a thirty-foot ladder to a small window high on the face of a building, and then threatening to shake the fellow to the street if he did not vote correctly, led an old, corrupt Republican boss to say admiringly, "When I saw what was within the scope of a reformer's vision, it was with sadness and humiliation that I realized the narrow limits of my own imagination."

The death blow to Buckley's regime came with this announcement: "Tuesday, November 10, 1891, will be remembered in San Francisco as a red letter day. It marks the indictment by the Grand Jury of Christopher Buckley, the notorious corrupt Democratic boss, and Samuel Rainey, his foremost henchman."

The Wallace Grand Jury, begun in Au-gust of 1891 to investigate the excessive corruption of the Republican-dominated state legislature, extended its probes to include the activities of the Blind Boss. Buckley returned to the city in July of 1891. But when he learned that the Grand Jury was interested in his affairs, he found that it was an auspicious time to take another vacation. On September 7, he left for the cooler regions of Canada and Europe. When questioned by newspapermen in Canada, Buckley vigorously denied leaving San Francisco because he was afraid of the Grand Jury. For reasons of health, he said, his doctors had given him orders to travel, "my sickness being an attack of nervous prostration."

Although he returned in 1894 and was indicted, the Grand Jury was invalidated on a technicality, and Buckley never was forced to account for his political sins. For the next six years he played only a minor role in politics. The decade of the 'nineties in San Francisco was dominated by the reformers, who struggled to find the means to responsible municipal government, only to be submerged and frustrated at the turn of the century by another colorful but different type of city boss. With the coming of the Australian ballot and a new primary law by 1900, Christopher Buckley vanished from the political arena. With him also vanished a unique era of political control: the age of the saloon boss. No better comment can be made, perhaps, than one uttered by the "Blind White Devil" himself: "Well, such is life and such is politics."

10
Henry George

California's literary past rings with the names of famous authors from Mark Twain to John Steinbeck. It is safe to say, however, that no California writer has ever had a greater impact on his generation than Henry George. His main work, *Progress and Poverty* (1879), is perhaps the most influential critique ever written about the American economic system. A Philadelphian who came to California in his teens, George was a man of many facets— journalist, economist, socialist, prohibitionist, white supremacist. His circle of admirers grew to include persons as diverse as Tolstoy, Shaw and Bryan. More trenchantly than any other person, George analyzed the ills of society in words that ring with the passionate indignation of an inspired reformer. His insights were fresh and his analysis revealed the mind of an original thinker. George's central concern was the growing gap between the rich and poor and the paradox of poverty advancing hand in hand with progress as the United States entered the industrial age as a burgeoning world power. His most important work was done during the 1860s and 70s as a struggling young journalist and father, toiling to support his family as the editor of several small California newspapers. This was an era when the state's best lands (her most valuable resource) were coming under the unscrupulous control of great syndicates, led by the Southern Pacific Railroad. In denouncing these new evils of land monopoly, George spoke not just for Californians but for a whole generation of Americans. Why, he asked, was the American Dream of equality of opportunity being subverted to build great new fortunes for the privileged few? Why was corporate monopoly replacing free enterprise? His controversial remedy, a confiscatory "single tax" on land rents, was never seriously considered by the nation's leaders. But his *criticisms* of the existing order were carefully studied by a widening circle of influential citizens. Henry George died in 1897, just before the great reform movements that swept America during the Progressive era. But the reformers of that later era, whether they acknowledged the debt or not, owed much of their direction to Henry George.

Below is an exerpt from *Progress and Poverty* in which George points out disadvantages inherent in the system of private land ownership. Do his arguments appear sound to you? If so, why has his single tax never been enacted?

Courtesy, The Bancroft Library.

Henry George

Was Henry George the most important and most influential spokesman we have had for the non-Marxist left? Did he proclaim a pragmatic program in order to realize the American Dream? Was he a world-famous writer in his own time? We should be wrong if we said no to any of these questions. There was a time, not long ago, when Henry George's name was a household word. Once known to men in every walk of life, Henry George has now passed into relative obscurity, despite the school founded in his name and dedicated to the teaching of his ideas. Since he is largely unknown to many whose liberal and general education should have made them at least superficially aware of his extremely important role in the literature and social or political economics of the closing decades of the nineteenth century and the early years of the twentieth, it may be difficult for many people to accept the late President Franklin Delano Roosevelt's statement that George was "one of the really great thinkers produced by our country."

The popularity of George's major work, *Progress and Poverty,* has been unrivaled in the whole of the literature of economics.

First published late in 1879, after the post-Civil War depression of the 1870's had struck even the booming state of California, it captured almost immediately the imagination of countless people throughout the world. It is not often in any age that a book on political economy becomes a best-seller and its author an international hero, but that is exactly what *Progress and Poverty* and its author became. In contrast to the depression-ridden 1930's, our present affluence has made many of us—if not all of us—forget the problems to which Henry George addressed himself, problems perhaps more complicated and pressing than ever. The irony of starvation and poverty amidst apparent world-wide progress and plenty has been recognized once again. Nearly a century ago, Henry George said he had the needed remedy.

Henry George lived less than sixty years, but when he died he had become a national hero and an international celebrity. His economic and social theories had reached

Excerpts from *Henry George* by Edward Rose; copyright 1968 by Twayne Publishers, Inc. and reprinted with the permission of Twayne Publishers, A Division of G. K. Hall & Co., Boston.

lands that were only metaphors to Whitman. If the American Dream was ever a reality, it was in the social philosophy of Henry George's rather transcendental political economy that it was made concrete and pragmatic. For the non-American, and for many Americans also, George's ideas were a restatement in applied economics of the meaning of the Declaration of Independence. His major works, particularly *Progress and Poverty,* influenced the economic structure of nations, such as New Zealand, Australia, and Denmark; writers, such as Shaw, Bellamy, Garland, Tolstoy, and Dewey; political figures, such as Sun Yat-sen; and political movements, such as that of the British socialists in the last twenty years of the nineteenth century.

George belonged to both Emerson's America and the ages of Jackson and Lincoln, but he proclaimed the decentralized democracy of Jefferson. In many ways Henry George is America; for, having grown up in Jacksonian and Emersonian times, he lived through the Civil War to survive its divisive effects and to mature as a thinker in an expanding America which was destined to become a world power by the end of the century.

During the years in which Henry George first began his life-long quarrel with vested interests, he had several insights into the problems that he felt beset society. One memorable occasion was his attempt to circumvent the Associated Press–Western Union combine as Eastern representative of the San Francisco *Herald.* In a letter dated February 1, 1883, to Father Thomas Dawson of Glencree, Ireland, he recalled the spirit that had moved him: "Because you are not only my friend, but a priest I will say something that I don't like to speak of— that I never before have told any one. Once, in daylight, and in a city street there came to me a thought, a vision, a call—give it what name you please. But every nerve quivered. And there and then I made a vow.

Through evil and through good, whatever I have done and whatever I have left undone, to that I have been true."

In his acceptance speech for his first New York City mayoralty nomination in 1886, he described what it was that made him pledge himself with such transcendental fervor to the reformation of society: "Years ago I came to this city from the West, unknown, knowing nobody, and I saw and recognized for the first time the shocking contrast between monstrous wealth and debasing want. And here I made a vow, from which I have never faltered, to seek out and remedy, if I could, the cause that condemned little children to lead such a life as you know them to lead in the squalid districts."

The realty of his New York vision and the loyalty he felt for his vow were given added impetus by his so-called Oakland "illumination." While editor of the Oakland *Daily Transcript,* George was riding one day in the foothills outside the town when he came through a casual meeting to understand vividly and concretely "the reason of advancing poverty with advancing wealth":

Absorbed in my own thoughts, I had driven the horse into the hills until he panted. Stopping for breath, I asked a passing teamster, for want of something better to say, what land was worth there. He pointed to some cows grazing off so far that they looked like mice and said: "I don't know exactly, but there is a man over there who will sell some land for a thousand dollars an acre." Like a flash it came upon me that there was the reason of advancing poverty with advancing wealth. With the growth of population, land grows in value, and the men who work it must pay more for the privilege. I turned back, amidst quiet thought, to the perception that then came to me and has been with me ever since.

Of course, those who gained control of the land early and could patiently wait made great profits with no exertion. When land passed into private hands, all improvement in the area in question went to enriching the landowner and not to the people who worked it or to the nation and the public to whom it truly belonged.

George added later . . .

Is it not universally true that as population grows and wealth increases the condition of the laboring classes becomes worse, and that the amount and depth of real poverty increases? . . . The explanation that as population increases there is a greater strain on natural resources, and that labor in the aggregate becomes less productive, does not suffice, for the economies of production and exchange . . . more than compensate for any greater strain on natural resources. . . . Why is it, then, . . . as population increases, and wealth increases, that the largest class of the community not only do not get any of the benefit, but become actually poorer?

. . . As population increases, land, and hardly anything else but land, becomes valuable. . . . Land ownership levies its tax upon all the productive classes.

What is the remedy?

To make land-owners bear the common burden—tax land and exempt everything else.

What I propose, as the simple yet sovereign remedy, which will raise wages, increase the earnings of capital, extirpate pauperism, abolish poverty, give remunerative employment to whoever wishes it, afford free scope to human powers, lessen crime, elevate morals, and taste, and intelligence, purify government and carry civilization to yet nobler heights, is—*to appropriate rent by taxation.*

In this way the State may become the universal landlord without calling herself so, and without assuming a single new function. . . . and every member of the community would participate in the advantages of the ownership.

Now, insomuch as the taxation of rent, or land values, must necessarily be increased just as we abolish other taxes, we may put the proposition into practical form by proposing—

To abolish all taxation save that upon land values.

Henry George's philosophy is essentially an American worldview, true to the tradition of the American Dream. He saw no reason why the entire world could not become—if men were willing—the promised land of milk and honey, like the fruitful and ever bountiful plains of North America. In fact, it was America's task to show how such promise could be fulfilled, since America had the greatest opportunity that any nation ever had had; it was America's task to lead the rest of the world, like a colossal Joshua, into the millennial actuality of that dream. George had hinted that he was Moses. Consequently, he continued to be simultaneously left and right of center; but very few people, whether followers of George or not, have the capacity to be politically left and spiritually right. It is the kind of non-conformity for which, as Emerson would say, the world whips men with its displeasure.

George's style reflects his message. It is biblical in its cadence, thus matching the frequent quotations from the Bible and the way in which his major work, *Progress and Poverty,* has been received and perpetuated. His style is aphoristic, yet ample—natural but eloquent. A prophet cannot fail to be quotable. The simple diction and the simple message must go together; furthermore, they must be capable of expressing complicated and abstract theory in concrete terms. George's rounded style matches his rounded philosophy. The religio-economic nature of his ideas is expressed in the simple and proverbial presentation of involved and logical argument. Clarity is what counts. George's advice to his son is not only the kind of advice which a well-trained newspaperman would give and which most would-be writers would do well to heed, but it also describes his own method: "The fault of most young writers is that they are too stilted. Always prefer the short ordinary words and the simplest phrase. And without being ungrammatical or slangy, try to write about as you would talk—so as to be easy and natural." It is good advice, and it is modern and American: the kind of method necessary for those who would catch the ear of the world.

Liberty was George's major theme. The spirit and the substance of his Fourth of July addresses in the decade that marked the centenary of the Declaration of Independence were echoed in the conclusion of *Progress and Poverty* that came at the end of that decade.

11
Andrew Furuseth

The history of the American labor movement has been marked by extraordinary violence. Much of it has involved the seamen and other maritime workers of California. By far the most instrumental figure in the organization of sailors in the early years of the union movement in California was a Norwegian immigrant named Andrew Furuseth. Here, Hyman Weintraub's scholarly biography describes the early years of Furuseth's long career as a seaman and labor leader. A tough and uncompromising spokesman for the rights of the sailor, Furuseth was as responsible as any other man for the passage of the LaFollette Seamen's Act of 1915, which for the first time extended the Bill of Rights of the United States Constitution to men at sea. The Crimp System, which Weintraub discusses in detail below, was one of the most vicious methods used to oppress workingmen in an age of unprincipled exploitation of labor. After experiencing the plight of the sailor under this system at first hand, Furuseth devoted the rest of his life to seeing that it and similar abuses came to an end. How closely can Furuseth's struggle be compared to that of Cesar Chavez? Do farm workers face the same kinds of difficulties that confronted the merchant seaman in Furuseth's time?

Courtesy, The Bancroft Library.

Andrew Furuseth

In front of Sailors' Union headquarters in San Francisco is a bronze bust of a man with a stern face and a long beaklike nose. Most of the seaman who pass the statue daily hardly recognize the name of Andrew Furuseth. The unfamiliar features might remind them of the American eagle or of Cruikshank's caricature of Scrooge in *A Christmas Carol*. But observers would be aware of something basically wrong in that impression. The forehead and the eyes—did they not belie the stern, uncompromising features? Surely the man was too much of a philosopher to fit the picture of the eagle or of Scrooge.

The bust is no enigma to those who knew and admired Andrew Furuseth. Furuseth was a tough fighter. His features, like those of his Viking ancestors, were carved by the harsh struggle with the sea and the land. His face was stern because one did not wrest life from the ocean or sustenance from the land with laughter. It was kindly and philosophic because Furuseth's struggles were never undertaken in his own behalf; he devoted his life to advancing the interests of the lowest, the most scorned section of society—the seamen.

Fanciful stories have been told to explain Furuseth's lifelong devotion to the cause of the seamen. According to one of these tales, Furuseth was stricken with a fever while sailing on the Indian Ocean in 1874. An unmerciful first mate demanded that he continue his regular duties, despite his illness. Furuseth, filled with anger and resentment against the mate, determined to kill him. But no opportunity presented itself, and when the fever had passed, Furuseth had time for a sober second thought. He realized that killing the mate would have been no solution for himself or for other seamen who were driven like slaves. Organization by the seamen, and organization alone, could improve their status; and so the young sailor vowed to devote his life to this work. He deliberately set his course for the United States, whose principles of freedom offered all the sailors of the world the best opportunity for emancipation.

This story could certainly have been true. Any sailor in the 1870's could have had such an experience. That Furuseth was the victim

By Hyman Weintraub. Originally published by the University of California Press; reprinted by permission of The Regents of the University of California.

of harsh treatment or that he saw others being victimized during his years as a sailor can hardly be doubted. But it is unlikely that he made his resolve to free the seamen of the world when he was only twenty years old and had been at sea less than a year. It was to be another eleven years before he joined with other sailors in the Coast Seamen's Union. Moreover, in 1874 Furuseth knew no country but Norway, and at that time his native land had no examples of workingmen organizing to improve their conditions.

Furuseth's background was like that of many Norwegians who followed the sea for a livelihood. His father, Andreas Nielsen, who worked in the peat bogs, married Marthe Jensdatter on April 17, 1846. The young couple lived in Graaberget until 1852, when they moved to a cottage in Furuseth, a village southeast of the town of Romedal, about fifty miles north of Oslo. Here Anders, the fifth child, was born on March 12, 1854. In accordance with Scandinavian custom, the boy was known by the name of the village in which he was born—Andrew Furuseth. In 1855 the family moved to Damstuen, where five more children were born. Nielsen's job there was to look after the locks of a dam. His income was too small to support such a large family, and the Nielsens suffered continuous poverty. Meals often consisted of potatoes dipped in herring sauce and bread made of tree bark and flour. To supplement this starchy diet, the father would hunt and fish. Although the diet was not appetizing, it did not impair the longevity of the family; the father lived more than ninety years, and six of the children more than eighty.

When Andrew was eight years old, he was sent to Romedal to live and work with Jonas S. Schjotz, a farmer, in order to relieve the family budget. The choice was fortunate, for Schjotz, noticing the boy's keen interest in learning, arranged for his admission to the private parish school. When An-

drew was confirmed in 1869, at the age of fifteen, the church register recorded, "knowledge good, fairly good condition." On June 2, 1870, he left the Schjotz farm and went to Oslo, where he remained for three years. For a time he clerked in a grocery store, and then entered a training school for noncommissioned officers in the hope that he might be admitted to the Norwegian equivalent of America's West Point. Despite coaching by his friends, he was rejected. But his keen interest in languages, developed while he was a student, enabled him to supplement his earnings by translating English, German, Dutch, and French.

In 1873 Furuseth joined the crew of the bark *Marie* out of Draman. It is easy to understand why a young man of nineteen, blocked in his ambition to become an officer, seeing no future in working as a clerk, and with only the slimmest of family ties, would turn to the sea. There he would find a life of adventure; he could see the world about which he had been reading; he could dream of commanding a vessel. From 1873 until August, 1880, when Furuseth arrived in California, he sailed on Norwegian, Swedish, British, French, and American vessels. He may have spent part of his time fishing on the Newfoundland banks. Although there is no record of Furuseth's experiences during those seven years, his familiarity with ports throughout the world suggests that he sailed most of the seven seas.

It is unlikely that Furuseth had any experience aboard a steamship. His attitude toward steamship sailors was typical of the old-time sailor who thought of them as second-class citizens of the sea. Long after the sailing ship had, for all practical purposes, disappeared as a commercial rival to the steamship, Furuseth still held that a sailor could get his best training on board a sailing vessel.

There are many accounts of life aboard a sailing ship, depicting it as either a floating heaven or a floating hell. The truth is that it was neither heaven nor hell, but a purgatory of unending monotony. Occasionally a storm, a shipwreck, or a rescue punctuated the tedium and called forth the best in each man; or perhaps a beating or a fight occurred, demonstrating the depraved depths to which these same men could sink. Most days at sea, however, followed one another in monotonous regularity. The sailor's adventurous life, in fact, was more myth than reality.

Although the seaman's daily tasks were not unlike those of workers on land, there were important differences in his situation. Primarily, his ship was not just a place to work; it was his home. The men with whom he worked were not merely fellow employees, but his social companions and his family. The second important difference was the relationship of the sailor to the master of the vessel. Other workers, when conditions became unbearable, could quit, either singly or in unison. Seamen had no such choice. As Richard Henry Dana put it,

> . . . what is there for the sailors to do? If they resist it is mutiny, if they succeed, and take the vessel, it is piracy. If they ever yield again, their punishment must come; and if they do not yield, they are pirates for life. If a sailor resists his commander, he resists the law, and piracy and submission are his only alternatives.

Such absolute power led to abuses. Seamen were whipped, beaten, kicked, clubbed for minor offenses or no offenses at all. It is true that such treatment was the exception, but so was the whipping of slaves. The fact remains that both the slave and the sailor were subject to beatings at the will of the master, who could administer them with almost complete immunity. This unlimited authority presented those who possessed it with a strong temptation to use it. The captain was a lonely man; except for the mate, he had no one to talk to on long voyages. He was a virtual prisoner in solitary confinement on his own ship. Sometimes a captain would take out his own bitterness on his men.

A favorite method was to get a man when he was at the wheel. While both the sailor's hands were occupied, the master or his mate would taunt the poor devil until he answered back. This provided the excuse and the opportunity to strike him. If the wheelsman was a big fellow, a belaying pin was used instead of fists. The victim was expected to clean up his own blood.

> If a sailor was killed, the captain or officer was not convicted. The record of the official log was carefully worded to justify any unusual act on the part of the authorities. Testimony was quickly suppressed or manufactured. Witnesses were easily disposed of in foreign ports. Sailors whose testimony was feared were promptly turned over to the boarding house keepers. After a short debauch, they were put on some vessel about to sail for another part of the world. It was always assumed that the punishment or even death, of a sailor was caused by his rebellion against his authorities. In many cases this was so, but it would be useless to deny that seamen were occasionally, if not frequently, brutally treated, and sometimes murdered on the high seas.

Although watch followed watch in uninterrupted monotony, the seaman knew that this apparent serenity was enforced by the brass "knuck," the bare fist, the boot, and the belaying pin. These weapons might never be used, but their threatening presence was always part of the sailor's consciousness.

If such cruelties were practiced, or even if the sailor suffered the mental indignity of being in an inferior social position, why then did he not leave the sea? It is difficult for the free man to comprehend the status of the slave. It seems so easy, so simple a solution, to get another job. But even when the sailor went ashore, he did not escape from bondage; he fell victim to another kind of tyranny—the system of hiring through boardinghouses and "crimps." Caught in the toils of this system, the average sailor was virtually penniless, with no place to stay except the boardinghouse that enticed him, and with only a seaman's skills to earn his living.

In essence, the system was an economic arrangement whereby a ship's captain, instead of hiring sailors individually, relied on a seamen's boardinghouse to furnish his crew. Since the boardinghouse master agreed to supply men when needed and since competition was keen, he often resorted to unfair tactics to get and keep seamen in his clutches. Obviously, the time to catch the sailor was when his vessel entered the harbor, and so the boardinghouse employed runners who went out in small boats to meet the ships. They climbed aboard and tried to convince the sailors to patronize their particular establishment. They were free in handing out drinks. They made promises of fabulous jobs ashore or of much higher paying jobs on other vessels. They compared the paradise of the city with the hell on board ship, with the prospect of days and perhaps weeks of tedious loading and unloading of cargo in port. They handed out a few more drinks. They spotted the leader of the crew and made him a special offer. When they were ready to go ashore, they had usually convinced some of the men to come with them. Each sailor who went forfeited his wages and whatever clothes and equipment he left behind, because he had deserted the vessel.

At the boardinghouse the sailor was provided with a bed, food and drink, cigars, and even clothes and supplies. If he ran out of money, the boardinghouse keeper extended credit; if he went on a binge, the keeper sobered him up; if he got into trouble with the police, the keeper had connections to "spring him from the brig." Most important, the boarding master always managed to find him a berth on some vessel.

For all these services the sailor paid dearly. When he came ashore, he was charged five dollars by the runner, a dollar for the boat, and another dollar for the wagon that took him to the house. There he paid five dollars per week whether he stayed one night or all week. He had to buy supplies for his next trip: five dollars for oils, some more for cigars, a tin plate, a pot, a bundle of matches, a plug of tobacco, and a straw bed. It was no secret that the sailor was overcharged for everything he bought, but the boardinghouse keeper and the clothier felt that they were justified because they sold on credit. The seaman dared not buy for cash at some other establishment since that might jeopardize his chance of getting a job.

To prevent a sailor from leaving without paying his bill, the boarding master had worked out a foolproof system. When the sailor shipped out, the captain gave the boarding master an advance on the sailor's wages to pay the debts he had run up at the house; or the sailor authorized an allotment to the boarding master, which was a lien on his future earnings. Maritime law provided that he could not sign over more than one month's earnings, but somehow he seldom owed more than that amount. On the other hand, he rarely got a ship until he had run up a bill equal to one month's pay. In fact, the seaman soon learned that the faster he got into debt, the more quickly another job would be found for him. The sailor who did not drink or squander his money, who dreamed of saving enough to buy himself a little farm, soon discovered that there were no jobs for him. The boardinghouse could keep him without any risk and there was no hurry to find him a ship.

Into this picture there entered a broker known on the water front as the "crimp." He was a middleman, analogous to an employment agent. Instead of dealing directly with the vessels, the boardinghouse often made arrangements with a crimp to ship its men. The crimp contacted the captains and obtained crews for them; he also employed runners to bring sailors to the house. He charged each sailor five dollars for a "chance"—the fee of the employment agent. In addition, the crimp made money by charging the boardinghouse for shipping its men when there was an abundance of sailors. In time of scarcity, he demanded "blood money" from the captain and a commission on everything the sailor spent at the clothier's and at the house. He made loans to seamen and collected advances both for himself and for the boardinghouse. The crimp might also be a boarding master, a clothier, or even a runner; what distinguished him was his middleman function. Of all the links in the system, the sailor hated the crimp most. From the boardinghouse he got food and drink; from the captain, wages; but from the broker he got nothing.

No matter how much they hated the crimps, most sailors could not escape from the system. Only when seamen were unusually scarce could a man get a job on his own initiative, even with a captain who knew him and had been pleased with his work. A few found their avenue of escape in advancing from able seaman to boatswain, then to third mate, and up the ladder to captain of the vessel. But for the great majority there was no alternative but starvation.

The system became so firmly entrenched because it had advantages for everyone—even for the seamen. Many sailors preferred to let the boardinghouse keeper find them jobs rather than to tramp the docks themselves in search of work. Relying on the system, the sailor had no worries. The boarding master was content with an arrangement that enabled him to keep his house full. His best means of attracting customers was to promise them jobs and to extend them credit.

The captain and the owner of the vessel were also satisfied with the system. A captain could not spend his limited time in port rounding up a crew, for he had many other things to do. It was more convenient to let the boarding master know how many men he needed. This arrangement, moreover, eliminated haggling over wages with individual seamen; the boarding master knew what would be paid and which men could be obtained for that figure. When sailors were scarce, he somehow knew where additional men could be picked up. Except for the few occasions when seamen were in such short supply that the boardinghouse keeper demanded a bonus, his services cost the captain nothing. In fact, a boarding master might even pay a captain for an agreement to take sailors from his particular house.

Under this arrangement a captain was not concerned about losing some of his crew. The same runner who took the men off had others waiting at the boardinghouse to take their places. If the ship was to be in port for any length of time, the captain would have to feed and pay a crew that he did not really need. Even if sailors were in high demand and he was later held up for "blood money," the expense would be more than offset by forfeited wages and by the savings made while in port. On a long voyage the amount of wages forfeited might be so substantial that captains were known to "work the men ashore." This was notoriously true of British captains. Before a vessel put into a harbor, discipline would become especially strict, the amount of work would increase, petty annoyances would be invented, and the food would become bad. If the sailors still stayed aboard, the captain would refuse to grant shore leave while working the crew long hours in port. It was an unusual sailor who could, under such circumstances, resist the blandishments of the runner.

The crimping system was of necessity a part of the experience of seaman Andy

Furuseth. When Furuseth left his ship in San Francisco in 1880, at the age of twenty-six, he went to a boardinghouse. For four years, as long as he stayed at the house, he had no difficulty in shipping. Then, motivated by a desire for greater privacy or the wish to break away from the clutches of the boarding master, Furuseth moved to a rooming house occupied by other Scandinavian sailors at 26 Steuart Street. When seamen were in great demand, he could still get a job, but in 1885 he walked the beach for six weeks without work. Furuseth, who had been sailing along the Pacific Coast for five years and was probably known to most of the captains, was hard put to find a berth without the aid of a boarding master. Imagine, then, the fate of a sailor who was a stranger to San Francisco.

During this period Furuseth changed from a deepwater sailor—one who voyaged to foreign lands—to coasting sailor and a fisherman. The sea was a means of earning a living. Since coastal sailors were paid more than deepwater sailors, and the chances of making a big catch of fish in the Columbia River promised greater returns than shipping to China or around the Horn, Furuseth settled down to what amounted, for a sailor, to a domestic life.

On the San Francisco water front, Furuseth found congenial company. He did not seek companionship in the sense of looking for a confidant or a bosom pal, but he liked to talk and he needed men with whom he could talk. In San Francisco he found these men, for fully 90 percent of the seamen in the coastwise trade were Scandinavians. Although Furuseth knew French, German, and English, there is little doubt that he felt more comfortable speaking his native tongue. He could have found the same concentration of Scandinavians in the coastal trade on the Atlantic or on the Great Lakes, but San Francisco had the further advantage of paying the highest wages.

Like most Scandinavian seamen, Furuseth probably sailed in the large, square-rigged vessels that hauled lumber from the forests of Washington and Oregon to the booming community in the south, Los Angeles. Sailors on these ships not only were expected to be excellent seamen, but they also had to be adept at loading and unloading lumber. For, unlike most seamen, the West Coast sailor did the work of the longshoreman. This important peculiarity explains the ferocity of Furuseth's later attacks on longshoremen on the Pacific Coast and throughout the world. The nature of the California seacoast and the type of products shipped made it necessary for the sailor to handle cargo. In the days of the hide and tallow trade, seamen were expected to take the vessel to a point close to a ranch where they could pick up the bundles of hides and transport them to the ship. Men on shore could not be hired to do the loading because it was not a year-round job, but would take only a few hours or, at most, a few weeks. The same situation existed in the lumber trade. Longshoremen were not waiting at each lumber camp at which the vessel stopped, and the sailors were expected to load the cargo. Although most sailors considered longshore work beneath their station, the Scandinavians on the West Coast realized the advantages it gave them: they were better paid; they were not laid off every time a vessel came into port because the captain had no use for them; and they developed skill in handling and stowing lumber which made them difficult to replace.

To make voyages profitable, it was necessary to carry a heavy load since little of value was shipped north. It was customary to fill the holds with lumber and then to load the deck until the water reached the deck line. Skilled men were needed to secure the load so that it would not shift at sea and cause the loss of both ship and cargo. Skilled seamen were needed to maneuver the vessel safely into port in San Pedro, San Diego, or Wilmington.

Quite often the men preferred to go

fishing in Washington or British Columbia. The work was harder and the hours were longer, but there was always the possibility of returning with a "nest egg." The sailor who turned to fishing left San Francisco with the fishing fleet in March or April. He signed an agreement providing for a minimum monthly wage, but in addition he was either entitled to a share in the total catch or was paid extra for every fish caught. If he were fortunate, he might be back in San Francisco in two or three months with enough money to last until the next fishing season. More often he would return in September or October, complain about his poor luck, and receive about the same pay as if he had been working in the coastwise trade.

Andrew Furuseth made several such fishing expeditions during his years as a coastal sailor. His last long voyage took him to Alaska, where a new salmon-canning industry was developing. Early in April, 1889, when he was thirty-five years old, he joined a crew of some 250 fishermen who were going to Nashagak to establish a cannery. At the time Furuseth reported that his trip "was as uneventful as a sea voyage generally is," but almost thirty years later he described a dramatic incident that occurred just before the vessel reached its desination. In the Bering Sea the sailors noticed clouds of black smoke coming from one of the holds, which was loaded with highly flammable materials needed for the cannery. As the vessel pitched and rolled in the rough sea, the sailors opened the hatches and began digging through the cargo; fanned by the wind, the fire could have turned into a holocaust. Fortunately, the experienced seamen discovered the source and extinguished a conflagration that might have sent them all to the bottom of the sea. Perhaps Furuseth could characterize such a voyage as uneventful because, like most seamen, he had already experienced similar fires.

Furuseth was not particularly impressed with Alaska. In a letter home he wrote:

> When we arrived here (probably early in May) the snow was just getting off the ground, and it has been keeping on getting off ever since. This is a strange country. It would be warm if the sun would but shine; dry weather if the rain would but cease; and money to be made if the salmon would but come in, but thus far—and the season is about over—the salmon have been scarce, at least, where we are. Should other places turn out the same, the salmon fishing must, I think, be considered a failure.

Furuseth probably sailed for short periods after his return from Alaska in September; he spent almost two months on the Columbia River in 1892. But in 1885 he had joined the newly formed Coast Seamen's Union and had soon become so involved in its affairs that he could not have spent much time on ships after 1889. Furuseth had long been outraged by the seaman's virtual slavery under the crimping system. He saw that sailors were victimized by everyone on shore with whom they were forced to come in contact. Everyone profited at their expense, and worst of all, there was little chance to escape. It was in character for Furuseth to turn to organization as a means of achieving freedom. Even if he had been concerned only with his own welfare, it is unlikely that he himself could have escaped from the system by rising to officer status. Although he may have served as boatswain occasionally, he fell short of the qualifications necessary for advancement in the sailing ship era. A boatswain had to be big and strong, and willing to use his fists and boots to drive the men to work. Furuseth was tall, broad-shouldered, muscular, and capable of handling himself in any contest of strength, but he lacked the willingness to use his physical prowess to drive men to work. Moreover, he must already have exhibited some of the characteristics that marked him in later life as a recluse devoted to reading and meditation. If he were working today on a road gang, his fellow workers would probably call him "professor"—if they dared. Captains looking for boatswains did not ordinarily pick the intellectual type. Men on shipboard were ruled, not by reason, but by force or the fear of force.

Andrew Furuseth always regarded himself as a sailor. Everyone who ever met him thought of him as a sailor. He looked and dressed, walked and talked like a sailor. He thought like a sailor. But from September, 1889, until he died in 1938, Furuseth earned his living principally on land.

12

Jack London

Jack London's short, turbulent career as a writer spanned the years of the early 1900s, a turbulent era itself. Born poor, fatherless and finally penniless, London grew up in the school of hard knocks. He rode the rails, shoveled coal, mined for gold in the Yukon and even ran with the oyster pirates of San Francisco Bay with his own boat and mistress at the age of 15. London's early struggles of survival left him a priceless legacy of story materials. By his mid-20s he was one of the most widely read and acclaimed authors in the world, as well as a rebel of literature and a dedicated socialist. His personal life, packed with adventures as exciting as any he ever wrote, was also full of domestic tragedy. There were two unhappy marriages punctuated by desperate bouts with alcohol. London apparently took his own life with an overdose of drugs in 1916 at the age of 40. Here is Irving Stone's impressionistic, sympathetic portrait of California's most colorful writer on the eve of his greatness at the beginning of a new century. Today, Jack London's works are still widely read, not only in America but throughout the world. Of all the writers of his era, he alone evokes the heroic qualities of the memorable characters he created.

Jack London

Quietly, reflectively, London made an estimate of himself, his work, his age, and his future. He had a strong gregarious instinct, he liked to rub against his own kind, yet in society he saw himself as a fish out of water. Because of his background he took to conventionality uneasily, rebelliously. He was used to saying what he thought, nothing more nor less. The hard hand of adversity, laid upon him at the age of ten, had left him sentiment but destroyed sentimentality. It had made him practical so that he was sometimes known as harsh, stern, and uncompromising; it had made him believe that reason was mightier than imagination, that the scientific man was superior to the emotional man. 'Take me this way,' he wrote to Anna Strunsky in the early days of their acquaintanceship, 'a stray guest, a bird of passage splashing with salt-rimmed wings through a brief moment of your life—a rude blundering bird, used to large airs and great spaces, unaccustomed to the amenities of confined existence.'

He had no patience with show or pretense. People had to take him as he was, or leave him alone. He wore a sweater most of the time, and paid calls in a bicycle suit. His friends passed the stage of being shocked, and no matter what he did, said, 'It's only Jack.' He catered to no one, played up to and sought favors from no man, yet he was loved and sought after because, as Anna Strunsky put it, 'To know him was immediately to receive an accelerated enthusiasm about everybody.' His words and laughter and attitudes vitalized those with whom he came in contact; his presence in a group brought that group sharply to life. He had an electric quality that sent a current through people, shocking them into wakefulness so that their bodies and brains came alive when he entered a room.

Perhaps the greatest passion of his life was for exact knowledge. 'Give me the fact, man, the irrefragable fact!' is the motif that runs through all his days and all his work. He believed in the physical basis for life because he had seen the hypocrisy, fraud, and insanity behind the spiritual basis. He wanted scientific knowledge to replace unreasoning faith; only through accurate and penetrating reason could the God of the Dark Ages be taken off the backs of men,

From *Jack London: Sailor on Horseback* by Irving Stone. Copyright 1938 by Irving Stone. Reprinted by permission of Doubleday & Company, Inc.

could He be dethroned and Mankind set up in His place. An agnostic, he worshipped no god but the human soul. He had learned how vile man could be, but he also had seen the mighty heights to which he could aspire. 'How small man is, and how great he is!'

He demanded virility in a man, first and always. 'A man who can take a blow or insult unmoved, without retaliating—paugh! I care not if he can voice the sublimest sentiments, I sicken.' A man without courage was to him despicable. 'Enemies! There is no necessity. Lick a man when it comes to the pinch, or he licks you, but never hold a grudge. Settle it once and for all, and forgive.' He had an open-handed generosity with his friends; he gave himself to those he loved without reservation, did not abandon them when they hurt him or made mistakes. 'I do not feel that because I condemn the deficiencies of my friends is any reason why I should not love them.'

The backbone of his life was socialism. From his belief in the socialized state he derived strength, determination, and courage. He did not look for the regeneration of mankind in a day, nor did he think that men had to be born again before socialism could attain its ends. He would have liked socialism to filter through gradually, without open revolution or bloodshed, and he was eager to do his part in educating the masses to take over their own industry, natural resources, and government. But if the capitalists made this evolutionary process impossible then he was ready to fight at the barricades for The Cause. What new civilization had ever been born without a baptism of blood?

Organically related to his socialism was his philosophic adherence to a combination of Haeckel's monism, Spencer's materialistic determinism, and Darwin's evolution, 'Nature has no sentiment, no charity, no mercy. We are puppets at the play of great unreasoning forces, yet we may come to know the laws of some of these forces and see our trend in relation to them. We are blind factors in the action of natural selection among the races of men. . . . I assert, with Bacon, that all human understanding arises from the world of sensations. I assert, with Locke, that all human ideas are due to the functions of the senses. I assert, with Laplace, that there is no need of a hypothesis of a creator. I assert, with Kant, the mechanical origin of the universe, and that creation is a natural and historical process.'

In his writing he hoped to follow in the footsteps of his master, Kipling. 'Kipling touches the soul of things. There is no end to him, simply no end. He has opened new frontiers of the mind and of literature.' He announced his revolt against 'that poor young American girl who mustn't be shocked or given anything less insipid than mare's milk.' The decade in which he had matured, the last decade of the century, had been its low point, a period of sterility and vacuousness in which the forces of Victorianism had ossified into control. Literature was bounded on all four sides by a Mid-West morality; books and magazines were published for a public that considered Louisa May Alcott and Marie Corelli great writers. Original work was difficult to do, only respectable middle-class or rich people might be written about, virtue always had to be rewarded and vice condemned; American authors were commanded to write like Emerson, to see the pleasant side of life, to eschew the harsh, the grim, the sordid, the real. The American literary leaders were still the pleasantly poetic voices of Holmes, Whittier, John Muir, Joel Chandler Harris, Joaquin Miller. American editors, who dwelt in the rarefied and chilly atmosphere of the high places, paid unheard-of prices for Barrie, Stevenson, Hardy, even went so far as to print the daring revelations (editorially castrated, of course) of Frenchmen and Russians, yet demanded of their American authors a repetition of the pseudo-romance formula with only a change in backdrop permitted.

A revolution was being carried on in Russia by Tolstoi and the realists; in France by Maupassant, Flaubert, Zola; in Norway by Ibsen; in Germany by Sudermann and Hauptmann. When he read the stories written by Americans, and compared them to the work of Hardy, Zola, Turgeniev, he no longer wondered why on the Continent America was considered a nation of children and savages. The *Atlantic Monthly,* high priestess of American Letters, had been printing the fiction of Kate Douglas Wiggin and F. Hopkinson Smith. 'It was all perfectly quiet and harmless, for it was thoroughly dead.' Well, 'An Odyssey of the North' would be out in a few days now; neither the *Atlantic Monthly* nor American fiction would be harmless and dead any longer. He determined to do for literature in his own country what Gorky was doing for the art form in Russia, Maupassant in France, and Kipling in England. He would take it out of the Henry James high society salon and place it in the kitchen of the mass of people where it might smell a little occasionally, but at least it would smell of life.

In American literature of the day the three unmentionables were atheism, socialism, and a woman's legs. He would play his part in destroying organized religion, in destroying organized capitalism, and in converting sex from something vile, ugly, and unmentionable into the scientific play of selective forces engaged in the perpetuation of the species. Nor did he intend to become a mere pamphleteer; he was above all a writer, a maker of literature. He would train himself to tell stories, so adroitly that propaganda and art would be indissolubly wedded.

In order to accomplish his fourfold purpose he decided that he would have to make himself one of the best educated men of the dawning century. To calculate what kind of start he had in his Herculean task, he looked at the books spread out on his desk and bed, all of which he was in the process of studying and annotating. Yes, he was on the right track: Saint-Amand's *Revolution of 1848;* Brewster's *Studies in Structure and Style;* Jordan's *Footnotes to Evolution;* Tyrell's *Sub-Arctics;* Bohm-Bawerk's *Capital and Interest;* Oscar Wilde's *The Soul of Man under Socialism;* William Morris's *The Socialist Ideal—Art;* William Owen's *Coming Solidarity.*

The clock in his mother's room struck eleven. There was only one hour left to the perishing century. He asked himself what kind of century it had been, what it had left behind for America, the America that had started in 1800 as a group of loosely affiliated agricultural states, had spent its early decades pioneering in the wilderness, its middle decades developing machinery, factories, spanning the continent, its closing decades amassing the greatest wealth the world had ever known . . . and along with its wealth and technological progress had chained the mass to their machines and their poverty.

But the new century, ah! that would be a great time to be alive. The resources, the machines, the scientific skill would be made to serve mankind instead of enslaving it. The human brain would be educated in natural laws, taught to face the irrefragable fact instead of being anesthetized by a religion for the weak and a morality for morons. Literature and life would become synonymous. The true soul of man would emerge in his art and literature and music, niceties which the triple monster of frontier, religion, and capitalism had strangled in childbed.

What a magnificent America would his sons' sons see one hundred years from this night as they sat at their desks and surveyed the century that had just passed! It would be his fortune to help bring about that new America. He would cast off the shackles of the dark century now closing;

he would refuse to wear the ugly high stiff collars that dug into men's flesh, and the ugly high stiff ideas that cut into their brain and made them miserable. He would turn his back on the antiquated ideology of the nineteenth century and resolutely face the twentieth, unafraid of what it might bring. He would be a modern man and a modern American. One hundred years from this night his sons and his sons's sons would think back to him with pride.

Flora's clock tolled midnight. The old century was gone. The new one was beginning. He sprang up from his desk, donned a turtle-necked sweater, put clasps about his trousers at the ankles, took out his bicycle, and pedaled the forty miles through the dark night to San José. What better way to begin the century than by marrying the girl he loved on its opening day? If his sons' sons and their sons were to think back to him with pride one hundred years from this night, then he had no time to lose!

13

The California Progressives

The political and economic crises of the 1970s have given rise to a profound skepticism among the American people about their leaders and the efficacy of the laws of the land. California's progressive reformers in the early 1900s faced a similarly imperfect order. Unlike many of today's advocates of change, however, they held strong convictions that the "system" could be improved. The reason for their optimism was an apparently workable program of laws and a belief that the people, if allowed to choose honest leaders, would do so. The aftermath of their reform labors gives us pause to wonder. The problems remain—corrupting vested interests more powerful than the old Southern Pacific machine; big labor unions seeking favors; noisy demagogues bent on fanning flames of prejudice; insensitive, inept and wasteful bureaucracies. In the selections below, George Mowry examines the backgrounds and the dreams of California's progressive reformers. He gives us a collective portrait of this remarkable group who, if they did not achieve their goals, nevertheless fought hard to bring many existing evils under control. By and large the California progressives were well-to-do members of the upper middle class, educated, experienced in public life and, above all, deeply concerned. How typical they were of reformers in other states at the time is a matter of continuing dispute among historians. Looking back, one might ponder how much good our reformers in California actually achieved. Did they simply complicate government with needless new laws? Or did they make government more responsible to the people? The progressives aimed to restore honest government by placing qualified, incorruptible people in office, and by amending laws to prevent a return of corrupt elements in the years ahead. To what degree did they succeed? Or were their hopes foolishly naive to begin with? Whatever our judgment 60 years later, the fact remains that no California reform movement before or since has stirred such wide concern for making government work for the people.

the Southern Pacific political machine in Los Angeles, and the other against the control of the Union Labor party in San Francisco. In the opening speech of the progressive crusade against the Southern Pacific in Los Angeles, Marshall Stimson voiced a fundamental principle. The three choices which confronted the voters of the city, he said, were between, "a government controlled by corporate interests, Socialism, or if we have the courage, unselfishness and determination, a government of individuals."

Although Rudolph Spreckels felt it necessary, in launching the graft investigation in San Francisco, to declare that this was not "a class question" between capital and labor but one "of dishonesty and justice," his very phraseology indicated that there was a third group interested in civic affairs with different public standards from those of either labor or capital. From that time until victory in 1910, progressive literature was critical both of politically organized capital and politically organized labor.

The progressive revolt was not only, or perhaps even primarily, a matter of economics. A few progressives had been hurt economically by the railroad and other semimonopolistic corporations; certainly shippers and farmers had been. But the progressive leaders were mainly editors, attorneys, small businessmen, and real-estate operators. Instead of beggaring these men, the railroad occasionally subsidized them, as Fremont Older pointed out. Moreover, this was not a period of depression: mass immigration into the state and the resulting spiral in real-estate values, the great oil boom, the coming of the movies, and the expansion of fruit and vegetable farming produced a wave of prosperity in California which lasted until 1913. If the progressive leaders saw a real and immediate threat from the large corporation to their own economic stake in society, it is not apparent from their letters and their speeches. No-

where did the California progressives suggest that the big corporation be abolished.

Not quite so much can be said of their attitude toward the labor union. Admitting in theory that the union was a necessary organization in the modern industrial world, the progressives' bias against labor was always greater than against the large corporation. Even the more radical progressives hoped that unions were only a "temporary expedient representing the necessity of one class standing against another" until the time the country got "beyond the questions of class and caste." Most progressives felt that unions could do very little economically for the working man. "The law of supply and demand," Chester Rowell observed, "applies to wages as well as to other prices." In the long run there was "no escaping" that law. Even where unions had demonstrably raised wages for their members, the progressives were sure that the benefits applied only to the few and really hurt the many. Unionism was "but a war measure to provide relative justice to a few." Many progressives could not see why the skilled laborer needed the union for economic purposes, since they considered him the "American aristocrat," who "got the highest wages . . . fixed his own terms . . . and constituted our only leisure class."

So long as organized labor was reasonably ineffective as an economic bargaining agent, the California progressives were inclined to view the movement more or less tolerantly. But as soon as labor aspired to a closed shop, Chester Rowell inveighed against this goal as "antisocial, dangerous, and intrinsically wrong." When the Johnson administration later considered a limitation to the issuance of labor injunctions, Meyer Lissner bitterly protested that if labor's legal status was changed the closed shop would soon be upon Los Angeles as it had been in San Francisco. Lissner was ready, he wrote to Governor Johnson, to let their entire reform movement go down the drain "rather than let Los Angeles be thrown under the sort of tyrannical domination of labor unionism that exists in San Francisco."

The progressive's prejudice against organized labor is further indicated by the fact that not one progressive leader was recruited from the ranks of the unions. In the midst of an early fight against the Southern Pacific machine in Los Angeles, Meyer Lissner wrote that while it was all right "to work through the labor unions" and get their support, he was against any publicity of the tactics. "It may react," he added. Lissner's attitude in 1908 contrasts strongly with his willingness three years later to cooperate with anyone, including the remnants of the old Southern Pacific machine in the city, to stop the challenge of the Socialist party, supported by organized labor.

Despite the attitudes of the Los Angeles group, the progressive opposition to labor on economic grounds should not be over-estimated. In the north, Fremont Older, Rudolph Spreckels, Francis Heney, William Kent, and Hiram Johnson were all supporters of labor unions even though they did attack the corrupt Union Labor party. Johnson had acted as counsel for several San Francisco unions, and for years Older's paper had been frankly prolabor. Both Kent and Heney felt that a large part of their political support came from the laboring ranks, and Heney remarked that it was wiser to trust the labor vote "to stand for what is right and decent in government" than it was to trust the businessmen. Returning from a vacation, Rudolph Spreckels found that the directors of his bank had voted to give $20,000 to the openshop fund of the San Francisco Chamber of Commerce. Spreckels risked his presidency to fight the action and succeeded only after two antilabor directors had resigned. With Chester Rowell and Irving Martin, editor of the Stockton *Record,* he went to labor's defense repeatedly when industry organized to break the unions and create an open-shop economy.

If there is some evidence to suggest that the progressive orientation against labor was partly economic in origin, what explains the progressive opposition to the Southern Pacific Railroad and its associated corporations? Disgruntlement with insufficient political rewards may have activated some of the older progressive leaders, who, according to Senator Works, had previously worn "the collar of the railroad without seeming irritation." And undoubtedly some of the younger men who later became progressives were incensed when their youthful and independent political efforts were defeated by the machine. But to ascribe the later reform zeal of this minor group to these early defeats begs the larger question. Why did so many young progressives originally engage in independent politics and why, when once spanked, did they not learn their lesson as so many generations of young men had before them, and either quit the game or make their peace with the machine? The answer does not lie entirely in the realm of immediate self-interest but in the broader reaches of human intellect emotion, and group psychology. Squarely to the point is the fact of the opposition of many progressives, including some of the very rich, not only to the priveleged corporations but also to great wealth, particularly if it had been accumulated by means they considered unsocial. As most of them later distinguished between "good" and "bad" trusts, so did they distinguish between "good" and "bad" wealth. Like a repentant sinner, William Kent opened his congressional campaign in 1910 with an apology for his wealth accumulated by land speculation and with a promise to use his fortune to wipe out the system by which he had accumulated it. Few, if any, progressives would have agreed with the novelist Boyensen that all efforts to achieve great wealth were a denial of beauty. But many of them did believe with Goldsmith that:

Ill fares the land to hastening ills a prey
Where wealth accumulates and men decay.

The California progressive, then, was militantly opposed to class control and class consciousness when it emanated either from below or above him. This was his point of opposition. What was his positive creed? In the first place this "rank individualist," as he gladly styled himself, was in most cases an extremely religious man. His mind was freighted with problems of morality, his talk shot through with biblical allusions. He often thought of the political movement he had started as a part of the "Religion Forward Movement." As early as 1903, A. J. Pillsbury, who was later to become a leading progressive, praised Theodore Roosevelt for coming nearer "to exemplifying the New England conscience in government than any other president in recent times."

But if the religion of the California progressive was old American in its form, much of its content was a product of his recent past. Gone was the stern God of the Puritan, the abiding sense of tragedy and the inherent evilness of man. As William Allen White later wrote, the cult of the hour was "to believe in the essential nobility of man and the wisdom of God." With an Emersonian optimism, the California progressive believed that evil perished and good would triumph. Sin may have been original, but it did not necessarily have to be transmittable. There was "no natural compulsion," William Kent wrote, "including the lust for blood, the savage passion for reproduction, and the cruder forms of theft that ought not to be overcome by education and public opinion." Under the influence of Darwinism, the rising social sciences, and a seemingly benign world, the progressive had traded some of his old mystical religion for a new social faith. He was aware that

evil still existed, but he believed it a man-made thing and upon earth. What man created he could also destroy, and his present sinful state was the result of his conditioning. An editorial in Frement Older's San Francisco *Bulletin* expressed this reasoning: "The basic idea behind this age of liberalism is the simple one that all men, prisoners and free, rich and poor, are basically alike in spirit. The difference usually lies in what happens to them." And from that one could conclude that when men were given justice, they would return justice to society. The progressive, then, not only wanted to abolish a supernatural hell; he was intent upon secularizing heaven.

But for the most part, the progressive was content with the basic concepts of the economic system under which 1910 capitalism awarded its profits and its pains. He firmly believed in private property, profits, and especially the competitive system and even acknowledged that the corporation and the labor union were necessary instruments of modern business. What the progressive did object to in the year of his triumph was not 1910 capitalism as such, but rather the ideological, economic, moral, and political manifestations which had arisen from that system. He was confident, at least in 1910, that no inevitable causal relation existed between that system and its social results. Moreover, he felt sure that the nexus between the great corporations and the government, on the one hand, and organized labor and government, on the other, could be broken. Once those links were destroyed, he was certain that most of the political corruption would vanish; once "special priviledge" was removed, the system would right itself and the individual again would be supreme in economics as well as in politics.

The California progressive, then, wanted to preserve the fundamental patterns of twentieth-century industrial society at the same time that he sought to blot out not only the rising clash of economic groups but the groups themselves, as conscious economic and political entities. But he sought to do all this, at least before he had actually taken power, without profound economic reform. "The people," Rowell observed sometime after the progressive victory in 1910, "elected Governor Johnson to get moral and political reform." The word "economic" was significantly absent from the statement. From today's vantage point, the progressive's aim of a capitalist commonwealth:

Where none were for a class and all were for the state,

Where the rich man helped the poor and the poor man loved the great,

may seem incredibly naive. His stress on individualism in a maturing industrial economy was perhaps basically archaic. His refusal or inability to see the connection between economic institutions and the rising class consciousness indicated a severe case of social myopia. His hope to avert class strife by political and moral reform alone were scarcely realistic. And paradoxical in the extreme was the coexistence of his own intense group loyalties with his strong antipathy to the class consciousness of organized capital and organized labor.

14

Luther Burbank

The name Luther Burbank is only vaguely familiar to most Californians today. "I think he had something to do with raising flowers and new kinds of fruit," is a typical response whenever his name is raised. Burbank's contributions to the fields of botany and horticulture were immense. Yet he was virtually self-taught in both of these demanding and specialized areas of science. Burbank's practical genius for developing new and productive hybrids of fruits and flowers in his orchards, gardens and greenhouses resulted from a boundless curiosity, uncanny intuition, luck, and, most importantly, hard work. Raised in Massachusetts, he followed relatives to California, settling in Santa Rosa in 1875. For the next 50 years he astonished the scientific world with his amazing ability to produce new and much better strains of fruits, vegetables, flowers and grasses. The seeds derived from these laborious experiments were sold to orchardists and nurserymen, among whom Burbank soon gained an enthusiastic following. As is so often the case, however, professional scientists remained skeptical a good deal longer, and to some of them, Burbank always remained a maverick, an eccentric outsider. With the publication of his seed catalogues during the 1890s and early 1900s Burbank became world famous and his Santa Rosa garden a stopping place for famous and ordinary folk alike. Lack of adequate patent laws at the time prevented Burbank from making a fortune out of his seed catalogues. But it is doubtful whether great wealth would have deeply affected Burbank's style of life. Up early, to bed late, he spent his hours in his gardens, painstakingly grafting sapling shoots from one kind of apple or walnut tree onto the branch of another, achieving a desired result about once in every thousand tries. From such toil came many of the tasty varieties of plant foods and beautiful flowers that Americans and peoples the world over take for granted today.

Courtesy, The Bancroft Library.

Luther Burbank

The fragile-looking genius of the garden was never dull. Indeed, he was one of the most intriguing human beings the world has ever known, with a personal magnetism so astounding it had an almost hypnotic effect on visitors. And what visitors he had! Thousands each year made the pilgrimage to his small town just to see where he lived and worked, and among them were the great—Edison, Paderewski, John Burroughs, Helen Keller, Mme. Schumann-Heink, Liberty Hyde Bailey, Jack London, William Jennings Bryan, Sir Harry Lauder, John Muir. . . .

Why was this? They called him the wizard of horticulture—a term he objected to and never got rid of—because there was something magical in his accomplishments.

Before Burbank, no one had ever created new plants to order, building them to fit a set of specifications as if they were houses or ships or boardwalks, depending simply on how the lumber that made them was sawed up and fastened together. Before Burbank, the techniques of plant breeding were known, yes, but until they were used with his confidence and dancing imagination, they were tools without handles.

Burbank not only did what others had never been able to do, but he made it exciting. And when he told about it, he knew how to tell it. He could remark of a tree, "I've grown a thousand kinds of apples on it"; or, "To find this luscious strawberry, I grew five hundred thousand new plants—and then made a bonfire with 499,999 of them"; or, "Do you know, I grew so thin a shell on these walnuts, the birds ate them off the tree like cherries." Burbank was a superb and natural showman. Largely because of this, he became the first horticulturist the whole world knew about, and remains the only one.

No one, including himself, knew how many new plants he made in his crowded experiment grounds during his fifty-year career. The conservative estimate is more than eight hundred, created or improved. To get the total, whatever it was, he had to make thousands of experiments, most of them ending in failure. And an experiment in this case was not a relatively brief perfor-

Luther Burbank by Ken and Pat Kraft (Meredith Press, N.Y., 1967), foreword IX-XII, pp. 72-79, and pp. 161-163. Used with permission of Hawthorne Books, Inc.

mance, but a drawn-out and extensive series of individual manipulations that might involve acres of plantings and often took years to complete. A testimony to his skill is that he kept as many as three thousand such experiments going on continuously all during his most productive years—and made such sketchy notes that he had to carry most of the details in his head.

Because he was what he was, Burbank's greatest gift to the world was the lasting one of having aroused a tremendous popular enthusiasm all over the civilized earth for the possibilities of horticulture. Dean Claude B. Hutchison of the University of California's College of Agricutlure said during the national Burbank centennial celebration of 1949:

> Devoting a lifetime to plant breeding, Burbank's plant improvements were almost without number; they include apples, berries of all kinds, cherries, nectarines, pears, plums, prunes, cactus, quinces, almonds, chestnuts, walnuts, grains, grasses and forage plants, beans, chives, corn, sorghums, peas, peppers, rhubarb, squashes, and tomatoes. His list of improved ornamental plants, including the well-known Shasta daisy to the production of which he devoted some seventeen years, is almost as long.

> But Luther Burbank's contributions to human welfare are not to be measured alone by the better plants he himself produced, important as they are. They are to be measured even more by the general interest in producing better plants which his life and work stimulated in the public mind, and in the widespread public interest and support for plant breeding which he aroused. In appraising his accomplishments, this awakened public interest must be given credit for having stimulated men and institutions into activities that have resulted in the advancement of the art of plant breeding more than those perhaps of any other man.

At times, Burbank, too, found the task close to impossible. With plant-patent protection he would never have had to worry about money and would in fact have been several times a millionaire. By means of his New England thrift and some sound investments, he did manage to accumulate an estate appraised at close to $170,000. The amount surprised many people who thought him much poorer. The sale of the business and of posthumous introductions eventually increased the estate to about a quarter of a million dollars.

The single most effective physical memorial to Luther Burbank is his garden, which the city of Santa Rosa remodeled at a cost of some seventy thousand dollars in 1960 as a small park covering about an acre, one quarter its former extent as an experiment garden. The property had been given to the city in 1955 by Mrs. Burbank, who also gave it the adjoining old Burbank homestead, in which she retained a life tenancy.

The garden, designated a National Historic Landmark in 1964, attracts as many as 70,000 visitors a year. The register shows the visitors come from all over the world. They see growing on this memorable acre such Burbank developments as a giant Paradox walnut tree, plums and a plumcot (a plum-apricot cross), mulberry, spineless cactus, the Burbank rose—a famous beauty of its day—Shasta daisies, lilies, tritoma, agapanthus, and other plants that flowered more beautifully or bore more richly under the famous Burbank touch. There is a display of some of his favorite garden tools, all of them built to his own design, and his old greenhouse and stable adjoin the garden. So does his unmarked gravesite, for he was buried at his own request in the cottage front yard, under a cedar of Lebanon he had planted.

When it came to talking about his work, Burbank never made any secret of his great device of mass production of plants, and it was during the 1890s that people grew vividly aware of and more and more fascinated by his bold manipulation of numbers.

Burbank's secret was the multiplication table. Where a scientist in a state agricultural experiment station of the time might be running three or four experiments, each involving perhaps two varieties of plants, Burbank would be juggling hundreds of separate experiments at once, each of them involving so many different hybrid plants, the brain reeled to contemplate it. Not all these experiments were on the king-size scale of, for instance, some of his berry work, but none was puny. The effect of all this trial and error on a gigantic scale was, oddly, gradually to build in the popular mind an image of Luther Burbank as the man who could make any plant do anything he wanted it to.

The truth is, he usually couldn't. Most of his efforts failed, and the reason he succeeded at all, when he did, was that he tried so many times that one try finally worked.

Another hazard to success was his own daring. Early in the 1890s he decided to see what he could do with the dewberry—not to get an improved dewberry but to use it as one parent in a series of off-track matings. For mates he chose other members of the dewberry's family, which is the Rosaceae. Since a plant family is a very broad classification, here are some of the relatives Burbank chose to try mating to his innocent dewberry: apples, quinces, pears, cherries, hawthorns, and strawberries. It was a startling assortment of crosses, and the surprising thing is that enough succeeded so as to provide him with seeds to raise five thousand little hybrid plants.

And what a motley assortment they were! Happily, about nine out of ten were as free from thorns as a pencil. Most were strong-looking, upright little things that promised to grow into something more like trees than bushes, and not one of them had leaves just like any other.

But then it turned out that most of these little hybrids wouldn't or couldn't bloom. That meant they couldn't bear fruit, which

cancelled them right out of the experiment.

Of the ones that did bloom, a mere two set fruit. Burbank eyed the tiny crop curiously, noting that the fruit of one plant looked like large pale blackberries, and that of the other, globular and purplish. Nothing that resembled apples, pears, or strawberries in the least.

But he could hardly wait to taste what he had. One good fruit well repays a long, hard effort with thousands of failures. As soon as the strange new berries were ripe, he bit into them—and was stunned to find them both absolutely seedless. To a housewife making preserves this would have been lovely, but to Burbank it meant he had come to a dead end. Without seeds to plant, the experiment couldn't go any farther. It is possible to propagate many plants vegetatively, as by rooting cuttings, of course, and Burbank could have done this with his new berries. The reason he didn't was that neither berry was good enough to bother with if it couldn't be improved by further breeding—which required propagation by seeds in order to bring out new characters. The final score:

Attempts:	5,000
Successes:	0

Because Burbank was naturally dramatic and was rapid at getting results, legends began early to build up around him. One of the milder ones alleged he was able to make his immense numbers of hybridizings only by gathering buckets of pollen and hiring gangs of Chinese to blow it onto the flowers with bellows. It was a good story in the Baron Munchausen tradition. Here's the way Burbank usually did the job:

A day or so before he was to cross one plant with another, he gathered the pollen from the male parent by cutting the pollen-bearing anthers out of its flowers and then tapping out the pollen onto a watch crystal when the anthers had dried a little. Pollen looks like very fine gold dust, and it takes very little to fertilize a flower. Even for a big job, Burbank could get all the pollen he needed from no more than a pint of blossoms. He found he could keep pollen for about a week, which took care of some possible gaps between blooming of the plants being crossed. It is essentially the procedure being used by plant hybridizers today, though by storing their pollen in a refrigerator, they are able to keep it viable longer than Burbank could.

Then when Burbank was getting ready to pollinate the female flower (commonly called the seed parent when hybridizing, since most flowers are both male and female and could serve as either pollen parent or seed parent) he did this: If it was a tree fruit he was going to hybridize, he would start by pulling off all but one tenth of the bloom buds, just as soon as they started to show a little petal color. This was to throw all the strength into the few remaining buds, and it also made it handier to work the tree.

Before he took the next step, which was floral surgery and consisted of cutting open the buds with a razor-edged knife, Burbank waited until he could hear the bees buzzing loudly in the tree. He always took his cue from nature, and here the bees were nature's time signal and meant the buds were almost ready to open. Since bees themselves would have instantly pollinated any open blossoms, these blossoms were never allowed to open.

Burbank and his helpers inserted their little knives less than halfway through each blossom near its base and made a swift circular cut that sliced out all the petals and the anthers, leaving the female organ, the pistil, naked and unharmed.

The last and most vital part of the job was to apply the pollen—and here it was the simplest operation of all. A camel's hair brush is often used, but Burbank simply dipped a fingertip in the pollen in a watch crystal and then touched a pistil. The pistil is sticky, and pollen acts quickly. It was a precise but fast part of the job, and Burbank's hands during hybridizing were once described as hovering like dragonflies over the blossoms.

Once pollinated, a flower is usually immune to other pollen, and Burbank seldom protected these hybridized blossoms—which, with their petals gone, were not apt to lure insects anyway. He did tag the blossoms, to keep track of what they had been crossed with, because except for an extra one or two for insurance, all he needed was one cross with each of as many different pollens as he had.

It was a part of Burbank's genius that he could keep the details straight on such a constant procession of changing factors and never lose sight of his goal. He added, in what may be classed as a tongue-in-cheek understatement: "When one considers that the cherry experiment is but one of a thousand going on at the same time, and the manipulation of millions of seedlings involved, some idea of the scope of operations is gained." It is also easy to understand why the Sebastopol grounds were off limits for most visitors: Ripening fruit is a great temptation to the passerby, and every piece of fruit in the experimental orchard had to be considered a potential winner until tested.

If you should wonder how one man could sample five hundred cherries and not take the fine edge off his taste buds long before the five hundredth, the answer is that he couldn't—neither Burbank nor anyone else. The "we" in Burbank's account above is not an editorial we but refers to helpers. He enlisted them from among his workers, from visitors, friends, anyone he thought capable of giving him a fair opinion of a fruit that did not disqualify itself from being tasted at all by poor shape, poor color, being diseased, or whatever.

Sometimes, when he thought he had something quite unusual in a fruit flavor,

Burbank would ask visitors to take a kind of blindfold test. His Bartlett plum was one such fruit he delighted in so testing. "Close your eyes and tell me what you're eating," he'd say, and hand them a piece of the plum. When they said, as they nearly always did, "A pear," his day was made. The plum even had somewhat the texture of a pear, and the tree looked something like a pear tree, but Burbank never claimed it was anything but one of the seedlings of a cross between two plums, the Kelsey and the Simoni. The large scale on which Burbank worked would have raised the chances of mutations—individual plants showing some sudden variations in established characters, due to molecular changes in genes, the heredity controllers—but nobody knew much about mutations at the time.

Though Burbank discussed freely at times his marvelous ability to pick from a thousand seedlings, the one good one for his purposes, he never pretended to know just what it was. He did say that his senses were so highly tuned that he suffered physical pain from certain music, was as aware of even faint odors as a fox, and could almost read print with his fingertips. He assumed his ability at selection was a sixth sense, especially because even persons he hired and who worked at his side for years never learned to do it.

In any case, given his wholesale plantings, followed by wholesale discarding, there was an enormous lot of plant material to be got rid of. Burbank could have sold some of his discards, and a great many people never did understand why he didn't sell at least the better ones and thus help pay for some of the expenses. The position he took publicly was an ethical one, refusing to "issue to the world a lot of second bests which will . . . clutter the earth with inferiority or mediocrity." Any businessman with a head on his shoulders would have agreed perfectly, from a sound merchandising standpoint: Every plant carrying the Burbank name was also risking the Burbank reputation.

Burbank's way of getting rid of all his also-ran plants was dramatic, as you might expect. He burned them; but instead of burning a little heap every day or so, he waited until he had a thing like a funeral pyre built up, and when he put the torch to it, the result looked like the Fourth of July.

These big fires were held at the Sebastopol farm, since it was out in the open countryside. The usual size of the pile was roughly twelve feet wide, fourteen feet high, and twenty-two feet long, or about the dimensions of a tall garage, and even professionally sophisticated horticultural visitors privileged to witness one of these great ten-thousand-dollar fires, as the neighbors called them, were impressed. Into such a blaze might go sixty thousand hybrid berry bushes, sizable two-year- and three-year-old plants, heavy with ripening fruit. Another fire might include, according to Burbank's own estimate: ". . . 499 cherry plants out of the 500 we have just made . . . 99,999 rose bushes . . . 1,500 gladiolus bulbs with a market value of half a dollar apiece, 20,000 cactus seedlings."

In 1899 the fourth *New Creations* catalog came out, and after a lapse of a year, the fifth and last appeared in 1901. After the original one in 1893, the others were considered supplements to it, and in addition to these, Burbank issued leaflets or slender booklets whenever he had something to justify the expense of this advertising, a practice he had begun in 1878, soon after he had started his nursery business. From 1901 on, he issued short or long booklets whenever needed. He used the familiar phrase *New Creations* in the titles of some, and two other recurrent titles were *Twentieth Century Fruits* and *Burbank Seeds*.

In the last year of the old century Burbank received another evidence of the intense curiosity he was arousing among scientists. He was visited by a large group of them who were in San Francisco for a meeting of the Association of American Agricultural Colleges and Experiment Stations. He far preferred such a visit to his addressing such a group. He never did get over his stage fright when facing an audience from a speaker's position, but he was an interesting and even fascinating conversationalist in his garden.

Whether he satisfied these 1899 academic scientists' curiosity is something else again. He had arrived at his results in his own way, and his way was not their way. Soon he was going to be making some very firm friends among university scientists, but he was not of their stamp, and he never would be. He was an exotic and brilliant creator, and his diversity was almost too great to be credited. When the new century go well under way, he would already have a tremendous record of achievements at what seemed breakneck speed: eighty new fruits, including besides his highly important developments in plums and prunes, new peaches, apples, quinces, and a long string of berries; dozens of new varieties within thirteen different classes of flowers, and even some new species, and one of the best new races of flowers ever fashioned, the Shasta daisies; besides which, he had developed a prolific new chestnut, had produced a 300 percent faster timber growth with two new walnuts, and had so far added to his tremendously successful potato three more new vegetables.

This was a performance so expert and so brilliantly versatile that it was literally a one-man Renaissance in horticulture. Here at last was the Ben Franklin of botany, the brilliantly versatile man.

15

Tom Mooney

Tom Mooney's sensational trial and long imprisonment represent a classic example of injustice and the most famous criminal case in California history. Mooney was a small time labor agitator, a self-styled social revolutionary who held no union office. A business-sponsored World War I Preparedness Day Parade on Market Street in San Francisco during the summer of 1916 provided the setting for Mooney's eventual frameup and conviction for mass murder. In mid-afternoon of July 22 a bomb exploded, killing ten of the parade watchers and injuring dozens more. A few days later Mooney and several others were arrested for the crime. Mooney, who had not been near the explosion, was sentenced to death on the dubious testimony of three witnesses in a trial that made a mockery of due process and attracted international attention. Only a worldwide outcry from socialists, labor organizations and humanitarian groups saved Mooney from execution, with President Wilson eventually prevailing on Governor William Stephens in 1918 to grant a last minute commutation of Mooney's death sentence to life imprisonment. During the 1920s and 30s, Mooney became a labor martyr second only to Sacco and Vanzetti as civil liberties groups battled against hostile public opinion in California for his acquittal. Finally, in 1939, after serving 21 years in San Quentin, Mooney was pardoned by a compassionate Governor Culbert Olson. Mooney's ordeal, better than any other event, exemplifies California's intolerant attitude toward anti-war sentiment and civil liberties during World War I. Mooney was also singularly unlucky. He faced an unscrupulous and politically ambitious district attorney bent on appeasing a public cry for vengeance. Also weighing against Mooney were two other facts: in 1913 he had been arrested for possession of explosives; and a week before the Preparedness Day bombing he had instigated an unsuccessful wildcat strike of San Francisco streetcarmen. These circumstances conspired to point the finger of guilt at the hapless iron moulder and rabble rouser. Who planted the bomb remains a mystery; no real effort was made to locate evidence once Mooney had been arrested. He was a handy scapegoat and he paid with 23 years of his life. Below, Richard Frost assesses the trial, its aftermath, and its meaning. Could something like the Mooney trial occur today, or are our civil liberties more safely protected against an angry majority than they were in Tom Mooney's day?

Courtesy, The Bancroft Library.

Tom Mooney

The San Francisco Preparedness Day bombing of July 22, 1916, interpreted at the time as the work of antimilitarist anarchists, was the origin of California's celebrated Mooney case. In an atmosphere of class tensions and hysteria abetted by irresponsible journalism, five local radicals were arrested and indicted for murder. Four were tried and two were convicted—Warren Billings and Tom Mooney. Billings was sentenced to life imprisonment, Mooney to death by hanging. During and after the trials, clear signs emerged of perjury, subornation of perjury, and the suppression of evidence by the prosecution. In 1917 Mooney became an international cause célèbre, a symbol of American capitalist oppression of militant labor. But Americans widely regarded him as a symbol of the radical threat to patriotism and to law and order during the First World War. In 1918 Mooney's sentence was commuted to life imprisonment, but the deeper issues of the case remained unresolved. For another two decades Mooney's name served as a rallying cry for radicals, organized labor, and defenders of civil liberties throughout the country, until Mooney and Billings were freed at last by Governor Culbert L. Olson in 1939.

The Mooney case never inspired novelists or poets. The verses of his admirers are best left to oblivion, along with Upton Sinclair's *100%* and a play called "Precedent," by Isadore J. Golden, a St. Louis lawyer. The able writers who cared about the case, like Sinclair Lewis and Dreiser, did not lend it their talents. Mooney often called for a Zola, but no Zola ever came. The case was too complex, the human qualities too mottled, to stir the artist's spirit. Unlike Bartolomeo Vanzetti, a radical humanist of deep sensitivity, Mooney was vain and repelled many of his own friends. Except for a few, including Finerty and Baldwin, those who knew him personally did not admire him. He was a small man of mixed clay. Moreover, there was no execution to heighten the tragedy. The injustice simply dragged to its tardy, untidy end, which came in political acts of justice, slightly soiled by the circumstances of politics.

The Mooney Case, by Richard H. Frost (Stanford University Press, 1968) pp. 488-491, Preface vii. Reprinted with permission of Stanford University Press.

The Preparedness Day bomber was never found. Over the course of many years, countless tips, some new accounts of the crime by alleged eyewitnesses, and a few confessions—including one from an inmate of a California state mental hospital—were given to the defense. Many leads were followed up, occasionally with a flurry of excitement and publicity, but none ever led to the solution of the crime. Various hypotheses were advanced to explain the bombing. One view, that the bomb had been planted by Mexicans in the heat of the United States-Mexican border fighting, was supported by eyewitness reports that one or two Mexicans had set down a suitcase at the spot where the bomb exploded. The most attractive hypothesis, however, was one put forward in 1920 by Baron Wilhelm von Brincken, who had been an attaché of the German Consul General in San Francisco in 1916, that the bomb had probably been a time bomb intended for one of the munitions vessels on the waterfront; in 1916 active German agents on the West Coast were sabotaging American munitions shipments to the Allies. Von Brincken speculated that an agent, making his way to the waterfront on foot, had been held up by the marchers, police barricades, and crowds, and had simply abandoned the bomb.

The Mooney case festered unresolved for more than twenty years, its causes widespread, its consequences pernicious. The trials and imprisonment of Mooney and Billings revealed dramatically the intolerance and injustice accorded radical dissenters before, during, and long after the First World War. The case, developing out of class social tensions and public anxieties accompanying the Preparedness Day crime, was forged through the repeated abuse of fair procedures by local law enforcement officials. It came ultimately to involve the inadequacies of the law itself (including the state constitution), the bias of the State Supreme Court, and the timidity of California's governors. The attitudes of Governor Olson's predecessors reflected public indifference and hostility to the defendants rather than the merits of the case. By and large, the public—particularly in California—preferred not to consider legal abuses and the law's inadequacies, but insisted that respect for law and order took precedence over the fate of two radicals.

A generation and more has passed since the freeing of Mooney and Billings. The law has changed since their days in court. In recent years the United States Supreme Court, preceptor to a reluctant nation, has handed down constitutional interpretations designed to compel scrupulously fair procedures in the prosecution of state criminal cases. Although these decisions have provoked widespread resentment ("There is no substitute for law and order," writes former Congressman Hamilton Fish, calling to mind the San Francisco *Examiner* of 1916), the Supreme Court has significantly advanced the centuries-old libertarian aim of English and American constitutional law—to protect the individual from zealous and unscrupulous exercise of authority. Under the leadership of Earl Warren, California's once intractable Attorney General who succeeded Olson as Governor before being appointed Chief Justice, the Supreme Court has made binding on state courts the provisions of the Bill of Rights essential to a fair trial. The Warren Court has required the prompt arraignment of criminal suspects; it has condemned incommunicado interrogation, and upheld the right of a suspect to counsel during police questioning; it has ruled that evidence illegally gathered in unreasonable searches and seizures is inadmissible in state criminal courts as in federal courts; and it has found that "massive, pervasive, and prejudicial publicity" attending a state trial may constitute a violation of due process. In all these respects, Mooney and Billings had been denied fair proceedings; and it is not too much to infer that had the United States Supreme Court established these same safeguards half a century ago, there would have been no Mooney case after the appellate courts had finished with it.

Moreover, if the California Supreme Court had subscribed to the principles of criminal procedure that it has recently upheld, there would have been no need to seek redress in the federal courts; for the California Supreme Court is one of the most libertarian state supreme courts in the nation, and in some respects has anticipated the Warren Court. For instance, it anteceded the Warren Court by several years in barring state use of evidence secured through illegal search and seizure. Since 1956 it has progressively established the principle of "criminal discovery"—the sharing of information by both sides before the trial—in order to minimize the sporting element in criminal trials and increase the likelihood that cases will proceed on their merits. A defendant in California now generally has the right to know in advance the names and addresses of prosecution witnesses, and to examine documents that may be used against him. Had such rules existed in 1916, they would have enabled Mooney's attorneys to obtain the Eilers Building photo-graphs before Billings's trial, and to make a careful advance check on Frank Oxman's assorted surprises.

For many years Mooney lacked access to the United States Supreme Court—access that has been available since the 1930s to many petitioners seeking protection of their rights in state criminal cases. The Mooney case itself contributed to the protection of these rights, by providing the occasion for expanding the writ of habeas corpus. Over the years since Chief Justice Hughes announced the Court's opinion, the Supreme Court has made *Mooney v. Holohan* bedrock constitutional law. The Court has cited the decision in more than fifty cases since 1935. In 1967, explaining a unanimous reversal of an Illinois rape-murder conviction (and death sentence), Associate Justice Potter Stewart said bluntly: "More than 30 years ago this Court held that the Fourteenth Amendment cannot tolerate a state criminal conviction obtained by the knowing use of false evidence. There has been no deviation from that established principle. There can be no retreat from that principle here." That principle, guaranteeing the constitutional rights of the accused, is a living monument to Tom Mooney and Warren Billings, and to those who defended them.

16

William Randolph Hearst

During most of his long life (1863-1951), William Randolph Hearst was California's most controversial and flamboyant personality—and quite probably its most influential citizen. Born and raised in San Francisco and heir to a huge mining and cattle fortune, Hearst overhauled his father's moribund San Francisco *Examiner* in 1887, and rapidly transformed it into the state's most outspoken and widely read newspaper. His formula for success was to entertain and shock his readers with gaudy crime exposes, social scandals, and crusades against foreign tyrannies or political corruption at home. This success formula was repeated over and over until Hearst's editorial voice became a national power. Through his control of a vast publishing empire he influenced public opinion significantly for two generations. Hearst's turbulent domestic life centered around his adulterous romance with Marion Davies, the chorus girl he transformed into a Hollywood movie queen. Hearst seemed in many ways a spoiled child—selfish, impulsive, blindly stubborn. He indulged himself by squandering his wealth on expensive memorials like his San Simeon estate, even while denouncing the income tax as millions went hungry during the Depression. Eventually his extravagances led the Hearst publishing chain to the edge of bankruptcy and he was forced to relinquish some of the dictatorial control over his minions. Whatever else may be said about Hearst, he represented the most powerful personal force yet felt in the history of American journalism. Following is biographer W. A. Swanberg's judicious assessment of the great man and his impact on his time. Was Hearst a truly great journalist or an irresponsible demagogue—or both?

William Randolph Hearst

When Hearst's body was flown to San Francisco, escorted by four of his sons, the plane passed directly over the San Simeon barony, a castle without a king. To San Francisco also flew Mrs. Hearst with her fifth son, John, from New York. Now that her husband was dead, she could resume in sorrow the position that had been hers in name only for decades. One could only guess at the thoughts of this intrepid little woman, still a seemingly ageless beauty, who had first known William Randolph Hearst a half-century earlier, at the time Miss Davies was born, had borne his five children, had held her head high and maintained her principles through years of separation, and now was still Mrs. Hearst in spite of it all, with the widow's mournful privilege of honoring her late husband and seeing him to his tomb.

The honors were great. People were gathering from all parts of the nation. Louella Parsons and Adela Rogers St. John met in the lobby of the Fairmont Hotel and went upstairs to have a "good cry." The body lay in state for a day and a half at Grace Episcopal Cathedral on Nob Hill (which Hearst had never attended since his mother's funeral), only a few blocks from his boyhood home. Hundreds filed past the costly bronze coffin to see the dead Hearst, clad in a dark blue suit, monogrammed shirt with cuff links, and a blue necktie woven with the family coat of arms. Some were the idly curious who had "heard all the gossip"; others were San Francisco *Examiner* and *Call-Bulletin* employes who had never seen the Chief in life but had heard stories galore about the strange requests he used to telephone to the city desk. Fifteen hundred persons heard the brief services read by the Right Reverend Karl Morgan Block, Episcopal Bishop of California, while a thousand more who could not get in waited outside. In Hearst plants all over the country, work stopped as employes observed a minute of silence—the last time the Old Man would stop the presses. Among the honorary pallbearers were the great or eminent—Governor Earl Warren, Mayor Elmer Robinson, Herbert Hoover, General MacArthur, Bernard Baruch, John Nance Garner, Roy Howard, Louis B. Mayer, Arthur Hays Sulzberger, Mrs. Fremont Older, Hugh Baillie and many others.

The competing newpapermen there—among them Howard, Sulzberger and Baillie—must have been repeatedly shocked over the years by Hearst's callous misuse of journalism. Others, such as Hoover, had personally felt the sting of unfair Hearst attacks. Two—Garner and MacArthur—had received virtually nothing but praise from the Hearst press.

All of them, as the bishop droned on, must have pondered the eighty-eight-year paradox that had come to rest in the bronze coffin in the nave—the career that had at times been marked by selfishness, presumption, ruthlessness, arrogance, cheapness and downright error to such an extent that the wonder was that they had gathered here to honor him. All of them, if they carried the thought through, knew they were not honoring his manifold error, or the millions he had given to charity, nor were they appearing here out of mere respect for the family. They were recognizing a character so prodigious as to be understood only as a flawed accident of nature that would never occur again—a personality of such titanic scope and torrential energy that it deserved recognition on that score alone, error or no error.

After the service, a police motorcycle escort led the hearse and twenty-two limousines to Cypress Lawn Cemetery at Colma, just south of the city. The huge, marble Hearst mausoleum, surrounded by other great San Francisco names, contained Senator George Hearst, died 1891, and Phoebe Apperson Hearst, died 1919. In the committal ceremony, Bishop Block read the church's service, then Hearst's own *Song of the River*:

> *For life was born on the lofty heights*
> *And flows in a laughing stream*
> *To the river below*
> *Whose onward flow*
> *Ends in a peaceful dream. . . .*

Then William Randolph Hearst joined his two immediate ancestors.

Miss Davies, who was not invited to the funeral, remained in Beverly Hills. "I'd thought I might go to church," she said, "but I'll just stay here. He knew how I felt about him, and I know how he felt about me. There's no need for dramatics."

Deadlines, the house organ of the Los Angeles *Examiner,* announced that the Hearst papers would continue unchanged. This was like saying, after lightning and thunder had ended, that the weather would continue unchanged. Nothing could be the same with the Chief gone. The Hearst press had entered a new era, and only one aspect of this was the fact that Miss Davies, who had received so many flattering puffs under the old regime, would go unmentioned in the new unless she really *made* news, as she soon would.

Hearst's will, filling 125 typewritten pages, disposed of a personal estate of $59,500,000. It provided for the creation of three trusts. One settled $6,000,000 in Hearst Corporation preferred stock on Mrs. Hearst, along with an outright grant of $1,500,000 in cash. The second, for the Hearst sons, contained a hundred shares of Hearst Corporation voting stock and also enough preferred stock to assure an annual return of $150,000, which the five could add to their already handsome salaries as company executives. The third, a residuary trust, was for charitable and educational purposes, the beneficiaries to be the Los Angeles Museum, the University of California, and others to be selected by a foundation Hearst provided for.

His sons were named as trustees of all three trusts. The will directed that a memorial be built to his "beloved mother" containing part of his art treasures, for public use. As executors of the will he chose eight of his executives, including Berlin, Huberth and Howey. True to his instinct for clinging to what he had, he begged his executors to keep the somewhat shrunken but still vast publishing empire intact: "I request my executors and trustees . . . not to part with the ownership or control of any newspaper, magazine, feature service, news service, photographic service or periodical . . . unless it shall, in their opinion, be necessary or prudent to do so."

There was no bequest to Miss Davies in the will. He had provided for her in an earlier trust fund, dated November 5, 1950. This gave her a lifetime income from 30,000 shares of Hearst Corporation preferred, the stock itself to revert to the sons upon her death. In the will he referred to her as, "my loyal friend, Miss Marion Douras, who came to my aid during the great depression with a million dollars of her own money . . ." He did his best to demolish the ever-recurrent rumor that he and Miss Davies had children, writing:

> I hereby declare that the only children I have ever had are my sons in this will named. . . . If any person or persons other than my said sons shall assert and finally establish . . . that he or she is a child of mine . . . then I give and bequeath to each such person the sum of one dollar. I hereby declare that any such asserted claim of heirship or kinship to me is and would be utterly false and wholly fraudulent.

A few days after Hearst's death, Miss Davies' attorneys staggered the executors by presenting an agreement by which Hearst pooled her 30,000 shares with his 170,000 shares and gave her sole voting power in the Hearst Corporation. This involved no further financial settlement on Miss Davies, but gave her something far more important—final control of the Organization. By its terms she would in effect succeed to the Chief's throne. This agreement reflected Hearst's knowledge that there was hostility toward her in the Organization, his fears that she might be victimized in the interminable legal unraveling of the estate, and his desire to protect her.

If there was one thing the executors were agreed on, it was to put an end to Miss Davies' influence and start the Organization out on a clean slate under professional direction. Yet it appeared that the only ground on which the agreement could be attacked was the ground that Hearst was incompetent when he made it. This was a line the executors were reluctant to take, nor did they relish the prospect of a long, expensive and bitter legal quarrel.

There was another way out. In his will, Hearst had admitted that he was without resources when Miss Davies loaned him a million dollars in 1937. According to California law, a husband could not give away community property. It might be judged that everything Hearst had earned since 1937 was community property, and Mrs. Hearst's lawyers, if they wished, could very likely exact the return of many of Miss Davies' possessions gained since that time.

There were tense meetings between attorneys for both sides. In the end, a compromise was arranged. Miss Davies agreed to relinquish all voting rights, and to serve the Organization merely as an "advisor" at a dollar a year.

The free delivery of Hearst papers to Miss Davies' door was then resumed.

At the time of Hearst's death, when every large newspaper ran a long obituary article, and the New York *Times* alone printed a summation of his career that totaled at least 20,000 words, they almost unanimously sidestepped hazarding any judgment as to his true stature. The Hearst press alone used such phrases as "the greatest figure in American journalism," which was true in a sense, but the Hearst press was emotionally involved and could not be expected to make a calm appraisal. The opposition press, which could be looked to for some sort of decisive opinion, just as one would expect an opinion of a deceased composer from fellow musicians, semed remarkably willing to suspend judgment. The New York *Times* likened him to "an elemental force," and said, "few persons ever succeeded in picking the lock of his character." The Los Angeles *Times* felt him similar to "a force of nature" that could only be described "as a physicist describes some phenomenon of the universe." The New York *Herald-Tribune* said, "one cannot assess (his) final influence." The San Francisco *Chronicle,* which had battled him for six decades, spoke of his "tremendous voltage," but backed away and added, "We would not try to outguess history and offer any final appraisal of William Randolph Hearst . . . But we know that he came into American journalism with both fists swinging, that American journalism will never be the same as it was before it felt his hurtling impact, and that the era has been a more colorful, more zestful time to live for his having been part of it."

The truth was, most newspapermen—even many who had hated and assailed him—were sorry to see Hearst go because a great, violent, fascinating chunk of life and news went with him. He was an original, unique, so unusual that no one was even remotely like him, the newsiest figure in the whole world of news, simultaneously the Sphinx and the blabbermouth of journalism. His passing left the scene strangely sedate and dull. The words "voltage," "impact," "force of nature" and "phenomenon of the universe" were telling descriptions of a man who was as powerful and unpredictable as a hurricane. They also reflected honest puzzlement. Hearst's own contemporaries were baffled. They were saying that he was great—somehow—but they could not explain why. The usual formulae for greatness did not work when applied to him. How could a man guilty of so many transgressions possibly be great? It was as confusing as adding two and two and discovering that for once it did not make four. Standards of appraisal which had never before failed were found wanting in the effort to measure Hearst, because so much of his greatness was obscured in error and misunderstanding.

The cautious obituarists must have known that Hearst's influence on journalism was mostly bad. For all his talk about editorial responsibility, he often forgot his own. He turned journalism into a mad, mass-production world combining elements of the peepshow, the Grand Guignol and the foghorn. True, he made millions, but he spent so many millions more that in 1937 he fell flat on his corporate face and would have been a bankrupt had not a group of executives and a war come along to save him.

Would it be wide of the mark to say that journalistically he was a failure?

As a politician, his chief contribution was probably a negative one. He courted voters with money and the greatest propaganda machine yet devised, but the electorate had the good sense to turn him down and vindicate the essential soundness of the democratic system. With his manifold flaws, he could have been dangerous in high office. Rejected, he still retained considerable power as a political oracle and an influence on voters, but he dissipated much of this because of the zigzag course he followed. In his later years he backed an unbroken succession of losers: Landon, Wilkie, Dewey, MacArthur. In fact, the public's refusal to follow him was so persistent that he himself was dogged by a sense of frustration, and it became almost axiomatic that the candidate he supported would lose.

Was Hearst, then, a failure as a politician also?

In his personal life, he had touched his own heart and the hearts of the two women closest to him—his wife and his mistress—with tragedy.

Was he a personal failure also? And if he was a failure as a newspaperman, executive, politician and husband, wherein lay his greatness and what was all the shouting about?

Indeed, Hearst, the noncomformist who

broke all the rules and led analysts a merry chase when he was alive, did it again when he died and confounded observers who tried to judge him by the usual standard of successes achieved. The effort to determine his real stature and put him in a proper niche could lead into obscure bypaths of psychic research and philosophy. Even today, a decade after his death and almost a century after his birth, the lock of his character is still unpickable. One gets only a partial view through the keyhole. Another clue can be found in what the obituarists did *not* say. They did not, for example, stress his unshakable integrity, his unswerving principles or steadfast beliefs.

These qualities he did not have. Had he had them—added them to his awesome vigor, industry, capability and intellect—he might well have been the greatest man of his era. He had integrity, on occasion. He had principles and beliefs which he firmly swore by at any given time but which could fluctuate as wildly as a compass near the pole. His crippling weakness was instability, vacillation, his inability to anchor his thinking to a few basic, rocklike truths that were immovable in his heart. The rocklike truths were missing in him. For all his potency of utterance, he seemed a creature of caprice, lacking real substance. Benevolent one moment, he could be malicious the next. The tragedy of Hearst was that he had all the equipment for first-rank eminence except the most vital ingredient of all. He was a Rembrandt struck color-blind, a Stradivarius out of tune.

Hearst, the worshiper of success, could not be properly measured in terms of success at all. His true splendor lay in fields not always associated with greatness—as a loser, a fearless fighter, and as an eccentric individualist.

He was unrivaled in the magnificence of his failure, the scope of his defeats, the size and succession of his disappointments. This was because he *tried* everything. In his six-ty-four years on the boards, he pleaded a thousand causes, dodged not an issue, feared not an enemy. His occasional successes were all but blotted out by the disasters he encountered. A lover of victory, he became instead a connoisseur of catastrophe. No one could dispute his title as the champion loser of his time. The inspiring thing about him was his ability to see himself trounced in one fight and to come back swinging in the next. Like a battle-scarred pugilist sent flying repeatedly to the mat, he won admiration by getting to his feet again and again, bloody but unafraid and still formidable. Hearst had taken scores of blows on chin and midriff that would have knocked out ordinary men. He kept coming back for more, sometimes forfeiting the admiration he won for his courage by his penchant for hitting below the belt. In the American democratic scene he was the eternal critic, dissenter and gadfly, and there was no one in sight who could come close to taking his place.

As an eccentric, a supreme screwball, a serio-comic vaudevillian who took the whole world as his stage and enacted there an endless series of fantastic charades for more than a half-century, no one could touch him. Always denied the lead role, he thundered out from the wings as a heavy or clown. Who but Citizen Hearst could have set himself up as king, owned seven castles, fought for the common man, looted the world of art, squired a bevy of actresses through Europe, chartered a plane to fetch shrimp, carried on a one-man war with France, rescued a toad and bewailed the death of a mouse? Who but Hearst housed two distinct personalities, swinging from one to the other so rapidly that one could never be sure which Hearst he would meet?

The thing that baffled the obituarists was that one obituary would not do for him. He needed two to describe his two selves. One would have to be decidedly unflattering:

Spoiled as a child, he never reached emotional maturity in eighty-eight years. He spent his life trying to gratify his overwhelming passions for wealth, power and position. Truth and principle seldom bothered him. His venomous attacks on those in office reflected his own envy and frustration. While he spoke piously of ideals in journalism, he left no gutter unexplored. He pushed the United States into war with Spain, sought to do the same in Mexico, but howled against wars that did not have his authorization. An immoralist, he assailed immorality in others. Aloof, driving, ruthless, he terrorized his own executives. In the depression, when Americans were starving, he squandered millions in self-indulgence and had the nerve to complain of taxes. When crossed, he could wallow in blind rage. Selfish, arrogant, distrustful of others, he thought himself so indispensable that he clung to the reins of his empire until death stiffened his fingers.

But the other obituary would show a different man:

Heir to millions, he had the character to choose work over idle luxury. He had many of the winning traits of a child. Shy, excessively courteous, he was so sentimentally soft-hearted as to be almost womanly. The kindnesses he performed for friends and employes were unnumbered. He could show the same concern for humanity in the abstract. His sympathies were so aroused by the plight of the Cubans that he insisted on saving them. He was so indigant at the exploitation of the common people that he became their defender against privilege. He never sat on the fence. He proved his patriotism by taking strong stands on issues which could not benefit him personally and in some cases lost him money and popularity. In one love he was true and devoted for more than thirty years. Wonderfully optimistic, he was also superlative in his sense of humor. He loved to do things for others, and many who received his bounty at his castles, on his yachts or on his group excursions to Europe and Mexico, still cherish his memory. He was tolerant of all religions. No miser, he believed in spending his money, keeping it in circulation, paying good salaries. He stood stoutly behind his editors and reporters, and if his executives feared him, they nevertheless venerated him. Gentleness and consideration were a part of his indefinable charm. Two of his warmest admirers were his valet of a quarter-century, George Thompson, and his horticulturist for thirty years, Nigel Keep. During the minute of silence when the presses stopped, thousands of Hearst employees knew that a titan had passed whose like would never be seen again.

Both obituaries are true, though irreconcilable if Hearst had been one man. He was two, a Prospero and a Caliban, and the lucky ones were those who saw only his angelic side.

17

A. P. Giannini

The most far-reaching innovations in American banking during the first half of the 20th century did not originate or emanate from Wall Street. They came from California and were the achievements of Amadeo Peter Giannini, the son of Italian immigrants. Born in San José in 1870, Giannini moved to San Francisco's North Beach district where, with the help of in-laws, he opened the little Bank of Italy in 1902. By 1950, this institution, renamed the Bank of America, had become the largest bank in the world. The key to Giannini's success was the new policy of branch banking, which brought banks out of the financial centers and into the neighborhoods, the suburbs, and the small towns of California. Giannini's institution catered particularly to small savers, offering security for deposits and modest interest returns for the first time to thousands of California families, many of whom had never used a bank before. Giannini's approach to banking thus tapped an enormous new source of investment capital which, with the help of new state banking legislation in the 1920s, enabled the Bank of America to far surpass its older and more conservative competitors. Soon, banks throughout the country were copying Giannini's financial strategies. In the short exerpt which follows, Marquis and Bessie James trace the beginning of Giannini's career. Their friendly biography of the man and the bank clearly place Giannini among the giants in the history of American finance. But critics of Giannini ask, who was helping whom? Didn't his many small investors help Giannini much more than he helped them?

A. P. Giannini

The largest bank in the world is not where most people would expect to find it. It is not in New York, which is the world's financial capital. It is not in London, which was the financial capital of the world for a hundred and fifty years, or until New York took the lead after the First World War. The largest bank is in San Francisco. This institution is the Bank of America. Its founder, A. P. Giannini, intended it to be a bank for the person of moderate means, or, as Giannini put it, "the little fellow."

Banks are safer institutions than they were in 1904, when Giannini entered the field, and they are immeasurably more useful to our economy. To this improvement the Bank of America (which until 1930 was called the Bank of Italy) has contributed more than any other privately owned banking institution, and Amadeo Peter Giannini more than any other banker.

Giannini was the greatest innovator in modern banking. The only other to approach his stature was J. P. Morgan, the elder. It is easier to contrast than to compare the services to society of these dissimilar men. Morgan was the banker for men of great wealth and for combinations of greater wealth. The locomtive fireman who worked on the railroad systems Morgan unified and the puddlers in the Morgan-financed steel mills never entered the great banker's consciousness; or his Wall Street banking house. Can you imagine J. P. Morgan carrying on a conversation with a track laborer? Giannini could talk to anybody.

As the Bank of America came up the House of Morgan declined. The times favored Giannini. The past helf-century has witnessed a leveling process, as far as money goes: less for the Haves and more for the Have Nots. Giannini said this was a good thing. He helped it along. On the other hand Morgan probably turned over in his grave.

Somewhat by accident Giannini became a banker at the age of thirty-four. He did not go into banking for the reason that men customarily go into that or any business—to make money for himself. Giannini was then worth between $200,000 and $300,000.

Abridged from pp. 1-2, 4-5, 7-10 in *Biography of a Bank* by Marquis James and Bessie Rowland James. Copyright 1954 by Bank of America N. T. & S. A. by permission of Harper & Row, Publishers, Inc.

His young family was growing up in suburban San Mateo. Theirs was a roomy, comfortable home, called Seven Oaks, which Giannini had bought for $20,000. That was all the money and all the home Giannini intended that he or his family should ever have. Seven Oaks was Giannini's home when he died in 1949, in his eightieth year, leaving an estate of $489,278. The depreciation of the dollar taken into account, that was less than he was worth when he opened the Bank of Italy.

Giannini did not reach his eminence unopposed. He organized the Bank of Italy because he was indignant at the neglect of North Beach, San Francisco's Italian colony, by other banks. He served North Beach so notably that he was able to set up prospering branches of the Bank of Italy elsewhere in the city. It was not, however, until he began to spread branches through the agricultural valleys of California and to storm the citadel of Los Angeles that the real struggle began. Branch banking was then a controversial issue. Its advantages to the depositor, the borrower and the stockholder were hotly disputed. The upshot was a long series of tussles with the regulatory authorities, state and federal. Laws framed for the protection of old-style banking stood in the innovator's path. But Giannini found, by legal means, ways around obstructive regulations and statutes.

The majority of the Bank of Italy's early patrons were immigrants who had never been inside a bank before. They had hidden their surplus cash under the mattress. When they borrowed they had usually borrowed from loan sharks at merciless rates. Giannini taught them the advantage of interest-bearing savings accounts. He would loan $25 at bank rates, often with no better security than the calluses on the borrower's hands. Very few San Francisco banks would loan as little as $100, in the belief that such small transactions were more trouble than they were worth.

After the earthquake and fire of 1906 the Bank of Italy was the first bank in San Francisco to resume operations. Its place of business was a plank laid across two barrels on the Washington Street wharf. Giannini's fortitude in that crisis and in the Panic of 1907, began to extend little Bank of Italy's reputation beyond the confines of North Beach. Going into the agricultural regions, Giannini accepted farm mortgages at 7 percent, against the going rate of 8 or more.

Giannini was born on May 6, 1870, in San José, in the San Clara Valley, fifty miles from San Francisco and near the southern end of San Francisco Bay. The birthplace was a twenty-room hotel that his father, Luigi Giannini, operated under a lease. This must have been something of an undertaking for a man of twenty-two who had come straight from Italy to learn the hotel business and the English language at the same time. When his son arrived Luigi had been married two years. The infant's mother, Virginia, was not quite sixteen. The young couple came from comfortably well-off farming stock near Genoa, their material circumstances attested by the fact that they had paid their passages to California and had enough left to take over the hotel. Few Italians arriving on the West Coast of the United States in that day were able to begin so far up the ladder.

Luigi Giannini did so well with the San José hotel that presently he was able to give up the place and move to forty acres he bought between the town and the bay. After six years on the forty acres Luigi was killed by a workman in a dispute over a debt of one dollar. The widow—twenty-two at the time of her bereavement—was the mother of three boys of whom the oldest, Amadeo, was seven. After carrying on alone for a time she married Lorenzo Scatena, twenty-six, whose capital was a team and wagon in which he hauled ranchers' produce to the dock at Alviso on the bay or to the railroad in San José. Lorenzo had worked his way from Italy before the mast. Amadeo Giannini was twelve when, in 1882, the family moved to San Francisco. Lorenzo Scatena had decided that more was to be made by marketing the produce of California's ranches than by growing it. At seventeen Amadeo was making buying trips for the firm. He toured the Santa Clara, the Napa and the Sacramento Valleys lining up commodities. The youth was a mixer and popular. He was liked by the ranchers, by the townspeople, by the rival buyers he met at nights in the country hotels. He worked longer hours than his colleagues. Soon the big San Francisco houses which for years had had standing arrangements with certain growers found L. Scatena & Company getting a share of the business.

By that time Amadeo Giannini was a young man of mark in San Francisco's Italian colony where he had a speaking acquaintance with almost everyone. In the near-by commission district he was regarded as "a live wire," and at times as "crazy with big ideas." An elderly lady of San Francisco remembers standing at her bay window on January 1, 1892. She saw Amadeo pass on his round of New Year's Day calls. He was six feet two. He wore a top hat, gloves and a Prince Albert. He carried a cane. The girl watcher thought: there goes the handsomest man in North Beach.

A call that Amadeo made that day was at the Bay Street residence of Joseph Cuneo, one of the Beach's rich men. Italian-born Joseph Cuneo had begun life in California as a miner but he found no gold. Opening a miners' supply store he had been ruined by an absconding employee. In San Francisco, however, his luck changed and he laid the foundations of a fortune in real estate. The object of the North Beach Brummell's visit to Bay Street was Joseph Cuneo's daughter, Clorinda Agnes. Before the year of 1892 was out she married him. Bride and groom were each twenty-two.

It was the death of his father-in-law in 1902 that decided A. P. Giannini's future. Joseph Cuneo left a fortune of half a million dollars, largely in North Beach real estate. Also he left a widow and eleven children, but no will. Nevertheless, the family decided to keep the estate intact for administrative purposes, and to place its management in the hands of A. P. Giannini for a term of ten years. Considering that sons of the deceased were grown and in business this unusual arrangement was a tribute to a son-in-law. By common agreement legal niceties were waived in the distribution of the estate's income, needy children receiving more than others. For his services Giannini was to get 25 percent of whatever increase there might be in the capital value of the estate during his stewardship.

Giannini's fee for ten years' work turned out to be $36,994. He had more than a hundred separate parcels of real estate to look after. There were also other holdings, among them shares in a little North Beach savings bank called the Columbus Savings & Loan Society. Joseph Cuneo had been a member of the board of that institution. Succeeding to his late father-in-law's place, A. P. Giannini began his banking career.

18

Louis B. Mayer

Louis B. Mayer's career seems the epitome of the American success story. The son of poor Russian-Jewish peasants who fled to America to escape a Tsarist pogrom during the 1880s, Mayer rose to become the highest salaried individual in the United States by the 1930s. As the head of Hollywood's largest studio, Metro-Goldwyn-Mayer, he became a cultural arbiter of the tastes of millions of American moviegoers. Mayer wielded his great influence during Hollywood's golden age at the box office, associating with the rich and the powerful—industrialists, royalty, statesmen, American Presidents. The exerpts below from Bosley Crowther's biography of Mayer give us a glimpse of the man at the height of his power. They reveal Mayer as a vindictive, sometimes petty individual, a poorly educated and often insecure person—a man ruthless in his dealings with his frequently unscrupulous competitors in the movie business. Many of the pioneer producers in the film industry were, like Mayer, immigrants of small means who took the lead in the development of the new form of entertainment when established business interests refused to risk the capital. The creative talent that Mayer and other producers brought to Hollywood helped to elevate the motion picture from its turn-of-the-century status as a lower class amusement to one of the great forms of entertainment, accessible to a worldwide audience. Typically, Mayer's relationship with his employees—writers, directors, actors—exposed the viewpoint of the businessman whose vision was inevitably limited by considerations of cost and by artistic and ethical standards that were not always the highest. This relationship underscores an ongoing dilemma of the movie industry: to what extent should the views of the producers who pay the cost impinge on the creative process of film making?

The persuasiveness of money in promoting power and prestige is not a peculiarity found only in Hollywood. Wealth often renders people potent wherever they happen to be. But the knowledge that Mayer was the highest salaried man in the United States—a piece of vital information annually announced through public prints by the obliging Treasury Department over a period of several years—made him loom ever so much larger than he already loomed in his realm.

Associates and competitors who had known him as a hardy executive and dynamic mover and shaker in group concerns of the producing industry now came to look upon him as something more than a local force. He assumed the impressive proportions of a national phenomenon. He was, in terms of salary, more productive and important than the presidents of big steel companies and captains of industry. This transmitted a certain grandeur to the business of making films and further elevated the level of Mayer's impressiveness and power.

He would have been a rare person if he had not canted a bit to the additional weight of importance that this evidence of money put on him. He was only human; he canted perceptibly. He was fully aware of the distinction of being the highest salaried man in the United States. And though he did not boast of it or use it to compel acquiescence to his desires, he did not discourage its being noticed as the proof of his Success.

Actually the secret of his income and the reason for his power in Hollywood was the fact that he controlled and administered the largest pool of creative talent in the industry. He had more actors, writers, directors, and other craftsmen under contract at Metro-Goldwyn-Mayer—more of the top ones in all categories—than were assembled in any other studio. And he had an uncanny shrewdness in manipulating this pool for the use of his own producers and for loan-outs and reciprocal deals from other studios.

In effect Mayer was in a position to dispense elements for the production of star-value pictures not only by his own company, but to a large extent by others. For, so often, others needed the stars or the writers or directors that were to be had only at Metro-Goldwyn-Mayer. At least they *felt* they needed them, as David Selznick felt he must have Clark Gable to play Rhett Butler, a key role, in *Gone With the Wind.* And it was Mayer's sharp skill in sensing the urgency of these needs and in cleverly trading upon them that gave him his overwhelming power. The heads of other studios might hate him. He was ruthless and tyrannical. But they respected his skill, and they admired him because they knew he was good.

He frequently crucified people. Francis X. Bushman was one who had early known the bitterness of his vengeance and the effectiveness of his Hollywood pull. Even though the distinguished actor had done a splendid job in *Ben-Hur,* he found himself strangely unwanted shortly after that film was released. On various illogical pretexts studio doors were closed to him and he was compelled to give up movies and seek his living on the stage.

Years later he learned the reason. Mayer had brought his family to see him in a play in Los Angeles at the time that *Ben-Hur* was showing. After the performance Mayer took his family backstage to greet the actor, and an inexperienced valet had refused to admit them to the star's dressing room. Mayer thought he was deliberately slighted. The boycott resulted.

From *Hollywood Rajah; The Life and Times of Louis B. Mayer* by Bosley Crowther. Copyright © 1960 by Bosley Crowther. Reprinted by permission of Holt, Rinehart and Winston, Publishers.

Late in 1940 the rising producer, Arthur Freed, brought William Saroyan to meet Mayer. Saroyan was, at that time, the newest genius in the American theater and the *enfant terrible* of the literary world. His short stories of West Coast Armenians (of which he was one) were all the rage, and his play, *The Time of Your Life,* a glittering compound of talk and tempest, had won the 1940 Pulitzer Prize.

Mayer was impressed by Saroyan, who had a great conversational flair and told him stories of Armenians that sounded to Mayer like stories of old Jewish families. "This is a bright fellow; we should have him," he later said to Freed. "But he doesn't want to work in pictures," Freed unhappily replied. This was a disposition that Mayer could not understand, so he suggested they bait Saroyan by offering him three hundred dollars a week just to come to the studio and look around.

The writer accepted the offer, but a few weeks later they found he wasn't picking up his checks, and then they learned he was at his home in Fresno, far from the lure of Hollywood. Freed urged him to write an original story in hopes that would bring him in, and three weeks later Saroyan delivered *The Human Comedy.*

Kate Corbaley, Mayer's favorite reader, reported that her boss wept three times when this little story was read to him. But Saroyan's price of three hundred thousand dollars semed a little high. He was asked to come to lunch with Mayer to work out a favorable deal. The latter offered fifty thousand dollars. "Tell you what I'll do," Saroyan said. "I'll toss you—a hundred thousand or nothing." "I can't gamble the company's money," Mayer replied.

They finally settled on sixty thousand as a suitable price, with the further provision that Saroyan would come to the studio at fifteen hundred a week with the idea of being groomed for a producer-director job.

The entertainment lasted only three months. Saroyan departed after having his fun and picking up the money that was generously paid to him. *The Human Comedy* was made, with Mickey Rooney playing the autobiographical role of a telegraph messenger boy in Fresno, which must have amused the author very much. Whether it amused Mayer is uncertain.

Saroyan's reaction to his experience was expressed shortly after he left in a piece published in *Daily Variety,* called "The California Shore-bird in its Native Habitat." In this thinly veiled excoriation of the processes of producing films, he summed up cryptically:

I left the joint also because sooner or later a man gets bored with bores, finaglers and jitney politicians. A man just naturally gets fed up with the baloney. He gets tired of witnessing the continuous and disgraceful crying, trembling and shaking. I made a net profit of one million (sic) at Metro. That is enough for any shorebird in the world, Orphan or otherwise.

Later he wrote a play which everybody recognized as a reflection of Mayer. It drew a devastating picture of a vicious egoist and was called *Get Away Old Man.* Considering the enthusiasm and high hopes that Mayer had for Saroyan at the start, this must have been extremely mortifying for one who put his trust in an Armenian.

Plainly the peak of personal triumph and glory for Louie Mayer was reached and maintained in the decade after 1938. For it was in these ten years that he was able to exercise and enjoy the authority, wealth, and personal freedom that he had battled all his life to attain. The deep-seated insecurity that had haunted his early years and had fed the fires of his aggressions, by which he steamed up his mammoth energy, had been sublimated more or less by the achievement of Success. Now he was on top, unchallenged, a Hollywood rajah in every respect.

He had his professional position, his supremacy as an earner of wealth, his increasing status as a national figure, and his mounting triumphs as a breeder of thoroughbreds. He was gaining an ever-widening circle of important and influential friends who were truly impressed by his vitality, expansiveness, and charm. As the most potent representative of the management corps in Hollywood he dazzled less glamorous industrial magnates with his air of possession of the place. Given his nature and background, it is no wonder that he spread out in these years as a supercolossal show-off and grandly self-serving egoist.

There was this about Mayer that was unquestioned and unusual among his ilk in Hollywood: he had a pronounced disposition and ability to make "big" friends. Thanks in part to his initial contact and experience with Hearst and to the rugged savoir-faire that he developed at functions in the Davies bungalow, he had a tremendous capacity to get through to people socially. He was also distressingly pervious to those who might want to get through to him.

The variety of his friends was mammoth. They ranged from Cardinal Spellman of New York, who was one of his finest and closest, to con men and even worse. Mayer and Spellman met when the prelate, who was then the auxiliary bishop of Boston, was visiting the studio in the company of Cardinal Pacelli, the Papal Secretary of State who later became Pope Pius XII. The two were attending a Roman Catholic Congress in Los Angeles in 1936 and included in their sight-seeing the "must-do" tour of Metro-Goldwyn-Mayer. With his usual attention to important visitors, Mayer showed them around and found an immediate kinship with Spellman because of Boston and the fact that the bishop had been an avid baseball player in Worcester at the same time Mayer was a fan in Haverhill. The two men saw each other thereafter and Mayer seldom missed a chance to call on Spellman, particularly after he became Archbishop and then Cardinal in New York.

Indeed it was often suspected and rumored in later years that Mayer would become a Roman Catholic because of his close association with the cardinal. There was nothing at all to these rumors. Mayer had deep respect for the Roman faith and a strong admiration for the organization, the discipline, and the rituals of the Catholic Church, but he had no wish to change his religion. And though he hobnobbed a good deal with priests, it is questionable whether the Church would have received him, even if he had wished. His domestic and marital record might have proved an embarrassment.

Religion was something that Mayer seemed to treat rather casually, anyhow, once he had pulled out of Boston and passed beyond the orthodoxy of his youth. Although he belonged to a temple, he rarely attended services, except on those days when it was virtually compulsory for an acknowledged Jew. He lived pretty much by his own standards, which were what was convenient at the time. Once he solemnly told a friend, in extenuation of his then rather reckless conduct, "The Talmud says a man is not responsible for a sin committed by any part of his body below the waist."

The fact was that the age he represented —the age of great expansion in American films, the era of the motion picture mogul— had passed several years before he died. Many and subtle changes in the film business after World War II had rendered obsolete and archaic the kind of monarchial management for which he stood. The stars could no longer be collected and controlled within his own galaxy; the market could not longer be engrossed with a massive output of glittering films.

Vainly Mayer sometimes insisted, "I want to rule by love, not by fear." Incredibly he never realized how passe was his point, "I want to rule."

The pitiful thing was that he pictured himself an endowed proprietor of the motion picture medium, and resented the preëmptions of younger men. He could not perceive the medium as a great, fluid cultural device, available for anyone to use it, like language or the alphabet. And thus, with others of his generation—or his age in the film industry—he saw change as a personal invasion, not as the promise of better things ahead.

Bitterness putrefied his last years, and the final shock to friends in Hollywood was the revelation of his dead hand making last vengeful slaps through his will, drawn for him in 1954 by a law firm he had not previously used. To his wife he left a modest fortune: $750,000 and their home. To his daughter, Irene, and his adopted daughter, Suzanne, the daughter of Lorena, he left $500,000 each. He also left sums to Irene's two sons, to Howard Strickling, and to his sister, Ida Mae. But he specifically directed that no legacy be given to his once adored Edith or her children. "I have given them extremely substantial assistance during my lifetime," the will sourly said. He likewise neglected to leave a bequest to his friend and doctor, Jessie Marmorston.

Ironically most of his fortune, which was ultimately checked out at some $7,500,000, a great deal less than it was thought to be, was left to the Louis B. Mayer Foundation, a fund for charitable purposes, presumably, but no instructions for its disposition were given the trustees, who were his widow, his business manager, Myron Fox, and his nephew, Gerald Mayer. Possibly he expected them to find some way to send it on to him.

Several relatives and other persons later contested the will. Thus the dismal contentions continued long after Mayer died.

Whether this was, indeed, intended by the violent, relentless man is a tempting speculation. He may have sensed, subconsciously, that he would be best remembered for his turmoils and inconsistencies.

The last time this writer called upon him, he took from his desk a card on which was printed a poem, and presented it with pride. The printed title of the poem was "The Man in the Glass," and these were the first and last stanzas:

> When you get what you want in your struggle for self
> And the world makes you king for a day,
> Just go to a mirror and look at yourself,
> And see what that man has to say . . .
> You may fool the whole world down the pathway of years
> And get pats on your back as you pass,
> But your final reward will be heartache and tears
> If you've cheated the man in the glass.

Perhaps he was thoroughly contended with the image he had of himself. Or that may have been the impression, the illusion he wanted to give.

19

Aimee Semple McPherson

This short selection on "Sister Aimee", by one of California's most distinguished writers, is part of a broader study of the phenomenon of evangelism in Southern California. The Southland has long been a hospitable place for enterprising evangelists. Billy Graham began his rapid rise as a gospel preacher in Los Angeles in 1949. But Graham's oratorical style and flair for the theatrical fall well short of the brand of fundamentalist religion preached during the 1920s and 1930s by the colorful, attractive woman from Canada. For twenty years Aimee McPherson radiated hope and zeal to the thousands who came to hear her. The elaborately staged sermons at her Angelus Temple in Los Angeles were spectacles worthy of Hollywood. Biographers have stressed the formative influence of her mother, an erstwhile Salvation Army worker. They also note that Aimee drew much of her following from among the lower middle class and especially older people recently arrived from the East. In her brand of salvation they may have found some fulfillment of their California Dream. McPherson was one of the first modern evangelists in her innovative use of radio and the press. She had a genius for self promotion and flourished on publicity. Her following, like that of her male contemporaries Billy Sunday and Robert Shuler, remained large and loyal in spite of the critics. Many clergy attacked her Four Square Gospel, with its parades and pageants, as blatant hucksterism—a mockery of true religion. But the people kept coming by the thousands, their contributions supporting the McPherson crusade through the grim years of the Depression until her death in 1945. In our era of revived concern for the rights of women, it is interesting to speculate on the part she might have played as an opponent of sexual discrimination.

Courtesy, The Bancroft Library.

Aimee Semple McPherson

Aimee, who was "not so much a woman as a scintillant assault," first appeared in California at San Diego in 1918. There she began to attract attention by scattering religious tracts from an airplane and holding revival meetings in a boxing arena. That Mrs. McPherson's first appearance should have been in San Diego is, in itself, highly significant. In San Diego she unquestionably heard of Katherine Tingley, from whom she probably got the idea of founding a new religious movement on the coast and from whom she certainly got many of her ideas about uniforms, pagentry, and showmanship.

Furthermore, San Diego has always been, as Edmund Wilson once said, "a jumping-off place." Since 1911 the suicide rate of San Diego has been the highest in the nation; between 1911 and 1927, over 500 people killed themselves in San Diego. A haven for invalids, the rate of sickness in San Diego in 1931 was 24% of the population, whereas for the whole country the sick rate was only 6%. Chronic invalids have always been advised to go to California, and, once there, they drift to San Diego. From San Diego there is no place else to go; you either jump into the Pacific or disappear into Mexico. Seventy percent of the suicides of San Diego have been put down to "despondency and depression over ill health." Curiously enough, Southern California has always attracted victims of so-called "ideational" diseases like asthma, diseases which are partly psychological and that have, as Wilson pointed out, a tendency to keep their victims moving away from places under the illusion that they are leaving the disease behind. But once they acquire "a place in the sun" in California, they are permanently marooned.

From San Diego, Mrs. McPherson came to Los Angeles in 1922 with her Four Square Gospel: conversion, physical healing, the second coming, and redemption. She arrived in Los Angeles with two minor children, an old battered automobile, and $100 in cash. By the end of 1925, she had collected more than $1,000,000 and owned property worth $250,000. In the early

Southern California: An Island on the Land, by Carey McWilliams (Peregrine Smith, Inc., Salt Lake & Santa Barbara, 1973), pp. 259-262, 1st ed. 1946. Used with permission of Peregrine Smith, Inc.

'twenties, as Nancy Barr Mavity has pointed out (in an excellent biography of Mrs. McPherson), "Los Angeles was the happy hunting ground for the physically disabled and the mentally inexacting . . . no other large city contains so many transplanted villagers who retain the stamp of their indigenous soil. . . . Most cities absorb the disparate elements that gravitate to them, but Los Angeles remains a city of migrants," a mixture, not a compound.

Here she built Angelus Temple at a cost of $1,500,000. The Temple has an auditorium with 5,000 seats; a $75,000 broadcasting station; the classrooms of a university which once graduated 500 young evangelists a year; and, as Morrow Mayo pointed out, "a brass band bigger and louder than Sousa's, an organ worthy of any movie cathedral, a female choir bigger and more beautiful than the Metropolitan chorus, and a costume wardrobe comparable to Ziegfeld's." Founding a magazine, *The Bridal Call*, Mrs. McPherson established 240 "lighthouses," or local churches, affiliated with Angelus Temple. By 1929 she had a following of 12,000 devoted members in Los Angeles and 30,000 in the outlying communities. From the platform of Angelus Temple, Sister Aimee gave the Angelenos the fanciest theological entertainment they have ever enjoyed. I have seen her drive an ugly Devil around the platform with a pitchfork, enact the drama of Valley Forge in George Washington's uniform, and take the lead in a dramatized sermon called "Sodom and Gomorrah." Adjutants have been praying, night and day, for thirteen years in the Temple. One group has been praying for 118,260 hours. While Mrs. McPherson never contended that she could heal the sick, she was always willing to pray for them and she was widely known as a faith-healer. A magnificent sense of showmanship enabled her to give the Angelus Temple throngs a sense of drama, and a feeling of release, that probably did have some therapeutic value. On state occasions, she always appeared in the costume of an admiral-of-the-fleet while the lay members of her entourage wore natty nautical uniforms.

On May 18, 1926, Sister Aimee disappeared. Last seen in a bathing suit on the beach near Ocean Park, she had apparently drowned in the Pacific. While Los Angeles went wild with excitement, thousands of templites gathered on the beach to pray for her deliverance and return. A specially chartered airplane flew over the beach and dropped flowers on the waters. On May 23, an overly enthusiastic disciple drowned in the Pacific while attempting to find her body. A few days later, a great memorial meeting was held for Sister at Angelus Temple, at which $35,000 was collected. Three days later, the mysterious Aimee reappeared at Agua Prieta, across the border from Douglas, Arizona.

Her entrance into Los Angeles was a major triumph. Flooded with requests from all over the world, the local newspapers and wire services filed 95,000 words of copy in a single day. Airplanes showered thousands of blossoms upon the coach that brought Sister back to Los Angeles. Stepping from the train, she walked out of the station on a carpet of roses. A hundred thousand people cheered while she paraded through the streets of the city, accompanied by a white-robed silver band, an escort of twenty cowboys, and squads of policemen. The crowd that greeted her has been estimated to be the largest ever to welcome a public personage in the history of the city. As she stepped on the platform at Angelus Temple, the people in the crowded auditorium were chanting:

Coming back, back, back,
Coming back, back, back,
Our sister in the Lord is coming back.
There is shouting all around,
For our sister has been found;
There is nothing now of joy or peace we lack.

The jubilation, however, did not last long. Working hard on the case, the newspapers soon proved that the kidnaping story, which she had told on her return, was highly fictitious. In sensational stories, they proceeded to trace her movements from the time she disappeared, through a "love cottage" interlude at Carmel with a former radio operator of the Temple, to her reappearance in Arizona. Following these disclosures, she was arrested, charged with having given false information designed to interfere with the orderly processes of the law, and placed on trial. Later the charges against her were dropped. During the trial, thousands of her followers gathered daily in the Temple and shouted:

Identifications may come,
Identifications may go;
Goggles may come,
Goggles may go;
But are we downhearted?
No! No! No!

Sister's trial was really a lynching bee. For she had long been a thorn in the side of the orthodox Protestant clergy who stoked the fires of persecution with memorials, petitions, and resolutions clamoring for her conviction. No one bothered to inquire what crime, if any, she had committed (actually she had not committed any crime). It was the fabulous ability with which she carried off the kidnaping hoax that so infuriated the respectable middle-class residents of Los Angeles. Miss Mavity writes that, in her opinion, it is "improbable that Aimee ever deliberately sought to harm another human being." Although I heard her speak many times, at the Temple and on the radio, I never heard her attack any individual or any group and I am thoroughly convinced that her followers always felt that they had received full value in exchange for their liberal donations. She made migrants feel at home in Los Angeles, she gave them a chance to meet other people, and she exorcised the nameless fears which so many of them had acquired from the fire-and-brimstone theology of the Middle West.

Although she managed to maintain a fairly constant following until her death in 1945 from an overdose of sleeping powder, she never recovered from the vicious campaign that had been directed against her in 1926. The old enthusiasm was gone; the old fervor had vanished. She was no longer "Sister McPherson" in Los Angeles, but merely "Aimee." In many respects, her career parallels that of Katherine Tingley: both were highly gifted women with a great talent for showmanship, both had lived in poverty and obscurity until middle-age, both founded cults, and both were ruined by scandal. In 1936 the Four Square Gospel had 204 branch organizations and a total membership of 16,000. More than 80% of her followers were city residents, mostly lower-middle-class people—small shopkeepers, barbers, beauty-parlor operators, small-fry realtors, and the owners of hamburger joints. Never appealing to the working class, as such, she had an enormous fascination for the uprooted, unhappy, dispirited *lumpenproletariat*. Over the years, many of her followers moved into the area around Angelus Temple, where they still reside.

20

Upton Sinclair

Upton Sinclair was one of the most prolific and long lived authors in American history. Raised in the East, he moved to Southern California in 1915 and became a leading spokesman for unfashionable causes. As California's most famous socialist, he wrote incessantly, crusading against the malignancies of big business, the weaknesses in virtually every form of American institutional life—from schools and churches to newspapers and labor unions. It is hard to select any single highlight from the career of so active and controversial a man—the author of more than 90 volumes and countless articles. But one would certainly be the publication of his most widely known work, *The Jungle* (1906), which detailed the plight of immigrant workers in the Chicago meat packing industry and brought major reforms in the food industry. The other was his only major political race—the 1934 EPIC campaign, during which Sinclair the socialist shocked the nation and terrified California Republicans by capturing the Democratic nomination in a landslide. What followed is recounted here by, of course, Sinclair himself in his absorbing autobiography, published in 1962. Reading his account here, do you think it would be possible for a socialist candidate like Sinclair to gain as wide a following today? Would the tactics and reforms need to be modified?

Courtesy of The Oakland Museum.

Upton Sinclair

I come now to one of the great adventures of my life: the EPIC campaign. There had come one of those periods in American history known as a "slump," or, more elegantly, a "depression." The cause of this calamity is obvious—the mass of the people do not get sufficient money to purchase what modern machinery is able to produce. You cannot find this statement in any capitalist newspaper, but it is plain to the mind of any wide-awake child. The warehouses are packed with goods, and nobody is buying them; this goes on until those who still have money have bought and used up the goods; so then we have another boom and then another bust. This has gone on all through our history and will go on as long as the necessities of our lives are produced on speculation and held for private profit.

Now we had a bad slump, and Franklin Roosevelt was casting about for ways to end it. In the state of California, which had a population of seven million at the time, there were a million out of work, public-relief funds were exhausted, and people were starving. The proprietor of a small hotel down at the beach asked me to come and meet some of his friends, and I went. His proposal was that I should resign from the Socialist Party and join the Democratic Party, and let them put me up as a candidate for governor at the coming November election. They had no doubt that if I would offer a practical program I would capture the Democratic nomination at the primaries, which came in the spring. I told them that I had retired from politics and promised my wife to be a writer. But they argued and pleaded, pointing out the terrible conditions all around them; I promised to think it over and at least suggest a program for them.

To me the remedy was obvious. The factories were idle, and the workers had no money. Let them be put to work on the state's credit and produce goods for their own use, and set up a system of exchange by which the goods could be distributed. "Production for Use" was the slogan, and I told my new friends about it. They agreed to every one of my suggestions but one—that they should get somebody else to put forward the program and run for governor.

I talked it over with my dear wife, who as usual was horrified; but the more I

The Autobiology of Upton Sinclair (Harcourt, Brace and World, New York, 1962), pp. 268-277. Used with permission of Upton Sinclair.

thought about it, the more interested I became, and finally I thought that at least I could change my registration and become a Democrat—quietly. It was a foolish idea, but I went ahead; and, of course, some reporter spotted my name and published the news. Then, of course, Craig found out and I got a mighty dressing down.

A great many people got after me, and the result was I agreed to run for the nomination at the primaries. I didn't think I could possibly win, and I was astonished by the tidal wave that came roaring in and gathered me up. I had no peace from then on; I carried the Democratic primary with 436,000 votes, a majority over the total cast for the half dozen other candidates.

So I had to go through with it, and Craig, according to her nature, had to back me. She would hate it for every minute of the whole campaign and afterward; but once I had committed myself, I was honor-bound, and quitting would be cowardice.

It meant dropping everything else, and turning myself into a phonograph to be set up on a platform to repeat the same speech in every city and town of California. At first I traveled by myself and had many adventures, some of them amusing, others less so. I had an old car, which had a habit of breaking down, and I would telephone to the speech place to come and get me. Once I was late and was driving fast, and I heard a siren behind me; of course, I stopped and told my troubles to the police officer. He looked at my driver's license before he said anything; then, "Okay, Governor, I'll take you." So I rode with a police escort blazing a mighty blast and clearing traffic off one of the main highways of central California. The phonograph arrived, and the speech was made!

I am joking about its being the same speech, because as a matter of fact something kept turning up and had to be dealt with. Our enemies continually thought up new charges, and I had to answer them. I would try to get them to come and debate with me, but I cannot recall one that ever accepted. That doesn't mean that I was a great orator, it simply means that I had the facts on my side, and the facts kept on growing more and more terrifying. The Republican opposition had no program—it never does, because there is no way to defend idle factories and workers locked out to starve.

Self-help co-operatives had sprung up all over the state, and of course that was "production for use," and those people automatically became EPIC's.

Our opponents would not debate; however, there were challenges from the audience, and now and then I would invite the man up to the platform and let him ask his question and present his case. That was fair play, and pleased the audience. There were always communists, and several times they showered down leaflets from the gallery. They called EPIC "one more rotten egg from the blue buzzard's nest." (The "blue buzzard" was the communists' name for the New Deal's "blue eagle.") When the shower fell, I would ask someone in the audience to bring me a leaflet, and I would read the text and give my answer. It was a simple one: We wanted to achieve our purpose by the American method of majority consent. We might not win, but if we cast a big vote we would force the Roosevelt administration to take relief measures, and we would have made all America familiar with the idea of production for use, both these things we most certainly did.

That campaign went on from May to November, and the news of it went all over the United States and even further. We had troubles, of course—arguments and almost rows at headquarters. I would be called in to settle them, but all I told anybody was to do what Dick Otto (my campaign manager) said. That brave fellow stood everything that came, including threats to kill him. There was only one thing he needed, he said, and that was my support. More important yet, he had Craig's. She never went near the headquarters, but when I was on the road, she spoke for me—over the telephone.

Sometimes she went to meetings that were not too far away. She always sat back toward the rear and was seldom recognized. At the outset of the campaign, at a meeting in a church, she observed that everybody sat still, and it occurred to her to applaud something I had said; instantly the audience woke up, and the applause became continuous. That was a trick she did not forget.

We had an eight-page weekly paper called the *EPIC News,* and I had to write an editorial for it every week, and answer our enemies and keep our organizers and workers all over the state alive to the situation. Sometimes Craig wrote for that.

A big advertising concern had been hired to defeat EPIC. They made a careful study of everything I had written, and they took passages out of context and even cut sentences off in the middle to make them mean the opposite of what I had written. They had had an especially happy time with *The Profits of Religion.* I received many letters from agitated old ladies and gentlemen on the subject of my blasphemy. "Do you believe in God?" asked one; and then the next question, "Define God." I have always answered my letters, and the answer to question one was "Yes," and the answer to question two was "The Infinite cannot be defined." There wasn't the least trouble in finding quotations from both the Old and New Testaments that sounded like EPIC, and it wasn't necessary to garble them.

When we carried the primaries, we were the Democratic Party of California, and under the law we had a convention in Sacramento.

Halfway through the campaign I wrote a little dramatic skit called *Depression Island.* I imagined three men cast away on a small island, with nothing to eat but coconuts. One was a businessman, and in the

process of trading he got all the coconuts and trees into his possession. Then he became the capitalist and compelled the other two to work for him on a scanty diet of coconuts. When the capitalist had accumulated enough coconuts for all his possible needs, he told the other two that there were "hard times." He was sorry about it, but there was nothing he could do; coconuts were overproduced, and the other two fellows were out of jobs.

But the other two didn't starve gracefully. They organized themselves into a union and also a government, and passed laws providing for public ownership of the coconut trees. The little drama carefully covered every point in the national situation, and nobody in that EPIC audience could fail to get the idea.

A group of our EPIC supporters in Hollywood undertook to put on the show in the largest auditorium available. I went to see Charlie Chaplin, who said he would come and speak at the affair—something he had never been known to do previously. I remember trying to persuade several rich people to put up rent for the auditorium. I forget who did, but there was a huge crowd, and nobody failed to learn the geography lesson—location of Depression Island on the map.

In the month of October, not long before election day, I made a trip to New York and Washington, I stopped off at Detroit and visited Father Coughlin, a political priest who had tremendous influence at that time. I told him our program, and he said he endorsed every bit of it. I asked him to say so publicly, and he said he would; but he didn't. He publicly condemned some of the very things he had approved, and he denied that he had given his approval.

In New York, of course, there were swarms of reporters. EPIC had gone all over the country by that time. I had an appointment with President Roosevelt at Hyde Park. It was five o'clock one afternoon, and some friends drove me up there. The two hours I spent in the big study of that home were among the great moments of my life. That wonderfully keen man sat and listened while I set forth every step of the program, and he checked them off one after the other and called them right. Then he gave me the pleasure of hearing his opinion of some of his enemies. At the end he told me that he was coming out in favor of production for use. I said, "If you do, Mr. President, it will elect me."

"Well," he said, "I am going to do it"; and that was that. But he did not do it.

I went to Washington to interview some of Roosevelt's cabinet members and get their support if I could. Harry Hopkins promised us everything in his power if we got elected. Harold Ickes did the same—the whole United States Treasury, no less. Also, I spent an evening with Justice Louis Brandeis—but he couldn't promise me the whole Supreme Court.

I addressed a luncheon of the National Press Club, and that was an interesting adventure. There were, I should guess, a couple hundred correspondents of newspapers all over the country, and indeed all over the world. I talked to them for half an hour or so, and then they plied me with questions for an hour or two more. I was told afterwards that they were astonished by my mastery of the subject and my readiness in facing every problem. They failed to realize the half year of training I had received in California. I can say there wasn't a single question they asked me that I hadn't answered a score of times at home. I not only knew the answers, but I knew what the audience response would be.

I had all the facts on my side—and, likewise, all the fun. I can say that EPIC changed the political color of California; it scared the reactionaries out of their wits, and never in twenty-eight years have they dared go back to their old practices.

In the last few days of the campaign, Aline Barnsdall, a multi-millionairess, came to Craig and told her she had decided to put ten thousand dollars into the fight. Craig told her to take it to Dick Otto, and needless to say she was welcomed at headquarters. Among other things we did with that money was to put on a huge mass meeting in the prize-fight arena in Los Angeles. I had never been in such a place before and have not since. Speaking from the "ring," I could face only one fourth of the audience at any one time, so I distributed my time and spoke to each fourth in turn. There were four loudspeakers, so everybody could hear, and the audience enjoyed the novelty. The speech was relayed and heard by an audience in the huge auditorium in San Francisco; so I dealt with the problems of southern California for a while and then with those of the north.

I remember on the afternoon before the election a marvelous noon meeting that packed the opera house in Los Angeles. Our enemies had made much of the fact that the unemployed, otherwise known as "bums," were coming to the city on freight trains looking for free handouts. This had been featured in motion pictures all over the state and had front-page prominence in the Los Angeles *Times*. I told the audience that Harry Chandler, owner of the *Times*, had himself come into Los Angeles on a freight train in his youth. I shouted, "Harry, give the other bums a chance!" I think the roar from the audience must have been audible as far as the *Times* building.

No words could describe the fury of that campaign in its last days. I was told of incidents after it was over. A high-school girl of Beverly Hills told me of being invited to the home of a classmate for dinner. The master of that home poured out his hatred of the EPIC candidate, and the schoolgirl remarked, "Well, I heard him speak, and he sounded to me quite reasonable." The host replied, "Get up and get out of this house.

Nobody can talk like that in my home." He drove her out without her dinner.

Another woman in Hollywood, a poet rather well known, told me of a businessman she knew who had made his will and got himself a revolver, and was going to the studio where I was scheduled to speak on election night; if I won he was going to shoot me. I did not win, and in my Beverly Hills home that night a group of our friends, including Lewis Browne, sat and awaited the returns. Very soon it became evident that I had been defeated, and Craig, usually a most reserved person in company, sank down on the floor, weeping and exclaiming, "Thank God, thank God!" Our dear Lewis, whom she knew and trusted, came to her and said, "It's all right, Craig. We all understand. None of us wanted him to win."

Many people rejoiced that night, and many others wept; I was told that the scenes at the EPIC headquarters were tragic indeed. I won't describe them, but will take you back to that old home in Greenwood, Mississippi, where an elderly judge sat listening to his radio set. It was Craig's Papa. He had owned a great plantation, much land, and two beautiful homes. He was the president of two banks, vice president of others—one of which he had founded; and in all of them he was a heavy stockholder. The panic had come, the banks had failed, and under the law he was liable to the depositors up to twice the amount of his own holdings. It had wiped him out. It should not surprise you to learn that he was hoping for his son-in-law's victory, and disappointed at his son-in-law's defeat.

21

Artie Samish

The agonizing demise of the Nixon Administration in the wake of the Watergate disclosures awakened many Americans to the urgent need for political reform at both state and national levels. Political corruption is hardly a new issue in American life. Here in California cynical political figures and an apathetc public created the climate for a new form of corruption during the 1930s and 1940s. The personification of that new power was Artie Samish. Born in Los Angeles and raised in San Francisco, Samish became the self-styled "secret boss" of California. Below, Samish deals all too frankly with the weaknesses of the political system he exploited. Samish's main theme is how he got and used power—through his control of selected members of a woefully underpaid and understaffed state legislature. One might assume after reading the following disclosures from the late lobbyist's autobiography that his system of "selecting and electing" candidates could have been stopped by paying legislators higher salaries and tightening laws governing campaign contributions. But would publicly financed campaigns and adequate salaries and staff make politicians immune to corrupting influences *after* their election? The revelations of Watergate seem to say no. Do these disclosures mean that corruption in American public life is ineradicable? As for Samish, he circumvented many of the laws of his day without actually breaking them. In so doing he achieved desired results for his privileged clients, often at enormous expense to the taxpaying public. Cannot the new and tougher laws now being enacted also be circumvented by new and more resourceful political operators? Samish wasn't the first malevolent figure to wield unwarranted influence in California politics. Nor is he likely to be the last.

Who the hell is Arthur H. Samish? You wouldn't need to ask that question if you had lived in California during the 1940s or 1950s. Or elsewhere, for that matter. During that time I became quite a famous character—some said infamous. I won't argue the point.

How did I get started on the road to such a position?

My first lobbying job came to me quite by accident in 1922. It might have been 1923—somewhere around in that time. In my wanderings around the capitol I had become acquainted with Jesse H. Steinhart, a very able and qualified attorney from San Francisco. For some years he had represented the S&H green trading stamps and the United Cigar Stores, which had their own trading coupons.

Steinhart's opponent was Frank Connolly, the lobbyist for the independent grocers of California. The independents didn't like the competition from the chain stores which gave their customers trading stamps with each purchase, and Connolly tried to get a law passed at each session of the legislature to ban trading stamps from California. Each session he was able to get the law passed, but Steinhart was able to get the governor to veto it.

I guess Steinhart had become rich enough that he didn't want to go on working for S&H and United Cigar. He seemed to think that I was an energetic and ambitious young man, and one day he asked me if I'd like to take over as lobbyist for the trading stamps.

"Sure—what the hell!" I replied. I was game to try anything.

I was just a green kid, but I leaped right in and started to learn the business. I had already gotten to know the legislators in my jobs as page, assistant history clerk, history clerk, and engrossing and enrolling clerk. But now I was in a new capacity. Now I represented the coupon industry, and I

needed to protect my clients. I had to know how the legislators stood on the trading-stamp issue. So I began talking to them. I had a little Studebaker then, and I drove it all over the state to see assemblymen and senators. I also called on the chain stores and trading-stamp people, the ones who were paying my salary. I convinced them to provide funds to help the campaigns of those legislators who were favorable to their cause.

That was to be the pattern for my future career as a lobbyist. First, organize the interest group and convince the members to contribute funds for their own interests. Then, spend the money wisely to elect those who would be friendly to those interests.

The system worked with my first clients. Never again did the legislature pass a bill against the coupon industry. Poor old Frank Connolly—I gave him and his independent grocers fits. There wasn't anything they could do to stop the trading stamps after I took over.

My achievement stirred up a lot of interest in this young fellow, Art Samish. A lot of people—important people—started coming to me for help and advice. I'd give it to them. But I was still learning, myself. I kept my eyes and my ears open at all times. I wanted to find out everything there was to know about the lobbying business.

To me, lobbying was not just a lot of backslapping and gladhanding. It was a business. I made sure it was fun, too, but primarily it was a business.

Some people didn't think lobbying was legitimate. Every few years they'd come sniffing around, expecting to find some

Taken from *The Secret Boss of California* by Arthur H. Samish and Robert Thomas. © 1971 by Arthur H. Samish and Robert Thomas. Used by permission of Crown Publishers, Inc.

hanky-panky. They never found any with me. I knew what the law said about criminal lobbying; it's right there in the state constitution: "Any person who seeks to influence the vote of a member of the Legislature by bribery, promise of reward, intimidation, or any other dishonest means, shall be guilty of lobbying, which is hereby declared a felony."

Bribery? Promise of reward? Intimidation?

That was for amateurs. It certainly wasn't for Art Samish. My method of delivering votes was the soul of simplicity. It was merely this:

Select and Elect.

That was all. I simply selected those men I thought would be friendly to my clients' interests. Then I saw to it that those men got elected to the legislature.

Select and Elect.

In that way I made certain that the bills I wanted for my clients won a friendly reception in the legislature. Sometimes an assemblyman or a senator might have disappointed me. Maybe he voted the wrong way on a bill I wanted. Too bad for him. I did my best to see that he didn't return to the legislature after the next election. And most times I was successful in that endeavor.

Select and Elect.

I didn't care whether a man was a Republican or a Democrat or a Prohibitionist. I didn't care whether he voted against free love or for the boll weevil. All I cared about was how he voted on legislation affecting my clients.

That was my job. I was being paid—and as the years went by, being paid a vast amount of money—to protect the interests of my clients. And I did so to the best of my ability. Judging from the results, that ability was more than adequate.

I wasn't alone in trying to influence legislation, not by any means. Sacramento was jammed with lobbyists for every legislative session. In 1949 the *San Francisco Chronicle* reported there were 364 registered lobbyists —and probably as many more who weren't registered. Being registered merely meant that you could appear before committees.

So in 1949 there were perhaps six hundred or seven hundred lobbyists in Sacramento, all trying to sway the votes of forty senators and eighty assemblymen. When you realize that each of those lawmakers was being paid one hundred dollars a month, you can understand why some of them might be swayed.

Naturally the legislators couldn't live on twelve hundred dollars a year. All had other sources of income, and they pursued their regular professions most of the time; by law, the legislature met only every two years (in time, special sessions made the period of service much longer than the writers of the state constitution intended).

Some of the legislators augmented their income by outright bribes from some of my lobbying colleagues, and occasionally they got caught at it. That was stupid, both on the part of the legislators and the lobbyists. There were other, strictly legal ways of adding to the income of the lawmakers and simultaneously making them friendly to your own organization.

Supposing the senator or assemblyman was a lawyer, as many of them were. Well, then you could see that the worthy barrister was hired on a retainer or received important cases on behalf of your clients. Or if Mr. Legislator engaged in the insurance business, you could assure him of some lucrative policies provided by your clients. It was all very simple.

Such practices were not uncommon with many of the lobbyists. Sacramento was swarming with lobbyists for every industry —oil, movies, gas, electricity, fishing, railroads, liquor, billboards, and so on. There were also lobbyists for every conceivable interest group—veterans, teachers, doctors, dentists, osteopaths, dog lovers, nudists. You can see why lobbyists were called the third house of the legislature.

In my early years in the third house, I was learning fast. My first really big break came in 1924, when Harry Regan and W. H. Pearson came to visit me. They were the owners of the Peninsula Rapid Transit Company, which operated bus service between San Francisco and San Jose.

"Art, the railroads are giving us all kinds of trouble," Harry said to me. "Do you think you can help us?"

"Well, I'd sure be willing to try," I told them.

I made a study of what their problems were. Mainly, they were getting clobbered by the Southern Pacific, which didn't like the buses competing for passenger travel. The S.P. had been pretty well discredited in Sacramento, but it was still strong in the little towns and cities where the railroad went through. These communities were convinced to place taxes on the bus lines. So a line like the Peninsula Rapid Transit might be paying taxes in Burlingame, San Mateo, Belmont, San Carlos, Redwood City, Palo Alto, and every other damn town it went through. That was a mess.

One little bus couldn't fight the railroads. But if all the bus lines got together, they could take on the S.P. and beat it.

I started talking to other bus-line owners —O. R. Fuller, who had a fleet of white buses in his Motor Transit Company of Southern California; Tom and Howard Morgan, who ran a bunch of stretched-out Pierce Arrows out of San Francisco; Buck Travis, who owned a line from Fresno to San Francisco. And a bunch of others. I convinced them of the wisdom of my plan, and they selected Arthur H. Samish as secretary-manager of the Motor Carriers Association.

After the appointment, Dr. Samish began diagnosing the patient's problem. The bus lines had to get out from under the tax squeeze of the local communities. I was able to convince the legislature to pass into law Section 50¼ of the Public Utility Act. That made all bus operations in the state full-fledged public utilities and placed them under the full and complete jurisdiction of the Railroad Commission (later called the Public Utilities Commission).

My next move was to place an initiative proposal on the ballot to give the bus and truck industry—I was now representing the truckers, too—the right to pay 4 percent tax in lieu of any and all other taxes. We had a fight with that one.

I tried to educate the voting public on the need for standard taxation for buses, pointing out that 1,700 small communities had no other public transportation besides buses. But the railroads wanted to crush the competition of the bus lines, and they campaigned against the initiative with propaganda and advertising. The measure was defeated by 70,000 votes.

Next time it was different.

I was going to beat the railroads at their own game. I convinced the bus owners to put up enough money for a first-class campaign. I hired a well-known cartoonist named Johnny Argens to draw a picture of a big, fat, ugly pig. Then I splashed that picture on billboards throughout the state with the slogan:

DRIVE THE HOG FROM THE ROAD!
VOTE YES ON PROPOSITON
NUMBER 2

I also had millions of handbills printed with the same picture and message. During the last weeks of the campaign they were placed in automobiles in every city and town. You'll note that I always spelled out "Number"; I never used "No." 2 because the voter might get confused and think he should vote "No."

The campaign worked. Boy, did it work! Nobody likes a roadhog, and the voters flocked to the polls and passed the constitutional amendment by 700,000! This was an amendment which I had managed to get through the legislature; it taxed bus lines at the rate of 4¼ percent and trucks at 5 percent in lieu of any and all other taxes. Not only that. The measure also provided free license plates for the buses and trucks.

All because the voters thought they were voting against roadhogs. That had nothing to do with it. Now what son of a gun but Art Samish could have thought of something like that?

During the 1930s, more and more organizations were coming to me with their particular legislative problems. Usually Dr. Samish could provide a cure.

One day a man from a San Francisco law firm came to me and said, "Art, we've got a problem."

"Well, you came to the right man," I said. "What seems to be the trouble?"

"Our client, the American Hawaiian Sugar Company has built a structure worth thirty to forty million dollars near the Carquinez Bridge. We checked the title to the property and we found out that American Hawaiian doesn't own it."

"That's quite some problem. Who does own the property?"

"The state of California."

"I see. And what do you want the doctor to do about it?"

"Anything you can. We need help."

They sure did. American Hawaiian had this big plant there in the tidelands of the San Francisco Bay, where all the big ships docked with the sugar. And they didn't own the property. They would have had one hell of a time moving the whole shebang.

I went back to Sacramento and I had a bill introduced in the legislature giving the director of finance power to enter into a lease with the American Hawaiian Sugar Company for the use of that tidelands property. When the bill got over to the assembly, I had the stipulation put in that the lease should be for sixty-nine years. I don't know

how I arrived at that figure; it just seemed like a good number.

That bill went through the legislature without a ripple. Not a ripple. I can assure you that the American Hawaiian Sugar Company was mighty relieved to have it passed. They expressed their gratitude in the form of a very large check for Dr. Samish's services.

Two years later, just so everything would remain safe, I introduced into the legislature a validating measure. That protected the lease from any future problems.

Was the legislature aware that American Hawaiian had already built a huge plant on that property?

I never concerned myself with whether the legislature was or wasn't aware of certain matters. My only concern was to take care of my clients. And I did.

After horse racing became legal in California in 1933, there was a lot of legislation which was important to the new racetracks. Dr. Charles Strub, the man who ran Santa Anita, realized this, and he hired the right man to look after his interests in Sacramento. I represented Hollywood Park, too.

For several years I made sure that Doc Strub's bonanza at Santa Anita wasn't tampered with. The state's pari-mutuel take remained at the same rate, and no new tracks were authorized. Santa Anita was assured of no serious competition.

It would have stayed that way except for Doc Strub's attitude. One day I was enjoying myself out at his race emporium in Arcadia when a messenger came to tell me, "Dr. Strub wants to see you."

I went all the way up to his cupola on top of the stadium, and Doc Strub started dictating to me what he wanted done.

When he was through, I stared at him for a moment. "You know, Charlie," I said, "I don't like you. That's going to cost you a hundred thousand dollars."

"What?" he said.

"That's right—a hundred thousand dollars. I quit."

I cost him a lot more than that. All of a sudden there was a different climate in Sacramento for racetracks, especially Santa Anita. The legislature started passing laws for a bigger take of the pari-mutuel betting. New racetracks were authorized, providing more competition for the established ones. And the state began clamping down on the outside investments of Santa Anita.

Doc Strub knew when he was licked. He whined, begged, pleaded for me to come back.

"Artie, I need you!" he said. "I may have to close the track if you don't help me!"

He sent his attorney to dicker with me. I told him I wanted a hundred thousand dollars, just like I told Doc in his cupola. We dickered and we dickered, and I let them off the hook for fifty thousand.

Suddenly the climate switched back in Sacramento. Once again Santa Anita got the kind of legislation it wanted, and Doc Strub could pack away his millions without undue interference.

22

Richard Nixon

In January, 1969, Richard Milhous Nixon became the first native Californian to assume the office of President of the United States. Five and one half years later, in August, 1974, he resigned in disgrace. The story of his rapid rise to the Vice Presidency and his narrow loss to John Kennedy in the 1960 Presidential election is dramatic enough. But his subsequent eight-year retreat into political limbo followed by an astonishing comeback and election to the Presidency in 1968 is one of the most improbable political odysseys of our time. His landslide re-election in 1972 by the largest popular majority in American history seemed, among other things, to reaffirm the American dream that a small town boy born of humble parentage could attain the world's most powerful office.

To many, Nixon, who grew up in the town of Whittier, in southern California, during the 1920's, embodied that elusive constituency known as middle America. He spoke for law and order, a strong defense against Communism, and reliance on individual initiative and free enterprise. These were Nixon's political stock in trade for a quarter century and they appealed to deep American sentiments and traditions. From the outset of his career, however, Nixon was despised by a substantial minority who saw in his political tactics the methods of a cynical opportunist. In addition, Nixon had his troubles with the press. As years passed, the tension between the two developed into an estrangement.

Then came Watergate and revelations of the most sordid and menacing political scandals in American history, with the President himself apparently near the center of the entire mess. Faced with almost certain impeachment and removal from office by the Congress, Nixon resigned in August, 1974. Although he received a full pardon from his hand-picked successor Gerald Ford shortly afterward, the amnesty was widely criticized. Nixon remained under a shadow of suspicion from which his reputation may never fully emerge, in spite of notable Presidential initiatives in foreign policy. To what degree the disclosures of Watergate have eroded public confidence in the Presidency and the American political system is not yet known. Below are exerpts from three of Nixon's more controversial public statements which reveal the man at critical junctures in his eventful career. How truthful was Nixon when he made these speeches? Did he believe his public statements? Why did his subsequent behavior so often contradict his promises?

Courtesy, The Bancroft Library.

The Checker's Speech (1952)

My fellow Americans, I come before you tonight as a candidate for the vice-presidency . . . and as a man whose honesty and integrity has been questioned. . . .

. . . I am sure that you have read the charge and you've heard it that I, Senator Nixon, took $18,000 from a group of my supporters.

Now, was that wrong? . . . I say that it was morally wrong if any of that $18,000 went to Senator Nixon for my personal use. I say that it was morally wrong if it was secretly given and secretly handled. And I say that it was morally wrong if any of the contributors got special favors for the contributions that they made.

And now to answer those questions let me say this:

Not one cent of the $18,000 or any other money of that type ever went to me for my personal use. Every penny of it was used to pay for political expenses that I did not think should be charged to the taxpayers of the United States. . . .

. . . Let me point out, and I want to make this particularly clear, that no contributor to this fund, no contributor to any of my campaigns, has ever received any consideration that he would not have received as an ordinary constituent.

. . . Now what I am going to do—and incidentally this is unprecedented in the history of American politics—I am going at this time to give to this television and radio audience a complete financial history; everything I've earned; everything I've spent; everything I owe. And I want you to know the facts. I'll have to start early.

I was born in 1913. . . .

. . . Well, that's about it. That's what we have and that's what we owe. It isn't very much, but Pat and I have the satisfaction that every dime that we've got is honestly ours. I should say this—that Pat doesn't have a mink coat. But she does have a respectable Republican cloth coat. And I always tell her that she'd look good in anything.

One other thing I probably should tell you, because if I don't they'll probably be saying this about me too, we did get some-

Abridged from pp. 117-120, 281-282, 314-316 in *Nixon: A Political Portrait* by Earl Mazo and Stephen Hess. Copyright © 1968 by Earl Mazo and Stephen Hess. Copyright © 1959 by Earl Mazo. By permission of Harper & Row, Publishers, Inc.

thing—a gift—after the election. A man down in Texas heard Pat on the radio mention the fact that our two youngsters would like to have a dog. And, believe it or not, the day before we left on this campaign trip we got a message from Union Station in Baltimore saying they had a package for us. We went down to get it. You know what it was?

It was a little cocker spaniel dog in a crate that he sent all the way from Texas. Black and white spotted. And our little girls—Tricia, the six-year-old—named it Checkers. And you know the kids love that dog and I just want to say this right now, that regardless of what they say about it, we're going to keep it. . . .

. . . You have read in the papers about other funds. Now, Mr. Stevenson, apparently, had a couple. One of them in which a group of business people paid and helped to supplement the salaries of state employees. Here is where the money went directly into their pockets.

And I think that what Mr. Stevenson should do should be to come before the American people as I have, give the names of the people that have contributed to that fund; give the names of the people who put this money into their pockets at the same time that they were receiving money from their state government, and see what favors, if any, they gave out for that.

I'm going to tell you this: I remember in the dark days of the Hiss case some of the same columnists, some of the same radio commentators who are attacking me now and misrepresenting my position were violently opposing me at the time I was after Alger Hiss. . . .

And now, finally, I know that you wonder whether or not I am going to stay on the Republican ticket or resign.

Let me say this: I don't believe that I ought to quit, because I am not a quitter. And, incidentally, Pat is not a quitter. After all, her name is Patricia Ryan, and she was

born on St. Patrick's Day—and you know the Irish never quit.

But the decision, my friends, is not mine. I would do nothing that would harm the possibilities of Dwight Eisenhower to become President of the United States; and for that reason I am submitting to the Republican National Committee tonight, through this television broadcast, the decision which it is theirs to make.

Let them decide whether my position on the ticket will help or hurt; and I am going to ask you to help them decide. Wire and write the Republican National Committee whether you think I should stay or whether I should get off; and whatever their decision is, I will abide by it.

Just let me say this last word: Regardless of what happens, I am going to continue this fight. I am going to campaign up and down America until we drive the crooks and Communists and those that defend them out of Washington.

And remember, folks, Eisenhower is a great man, believe me. He is a great man. . . .

"You Won't Have Nixon to Kick Around" (Nov., 1962)

And as I leave the press, all I can say is this: For 16 years, ever since the Hiss case, you've had a lot of—a lot of fun—that you've had an opportunity to attack me and I think I've given as good as I've taken. It was carried right up to the last day.

I made a talk on television, a talk in which I made a flub—one of the few that I make, not because I'm so good on television but because I've done it a long time. I made a flub in which I said I was running for Governor of the United States. The Los Angeles *Times* dutifully reported that.

Mr. Brown the last day made a flub—a flub, incidentally, to the great credit of television that was reported—I don't say this bitterly—in which he said, "I hope everybody wins. You vote the straight Democratic ticket, including Senator Kuchel." I was glad to hear him say it, because I was for Kuchel all the way. The Los Angeles *Times* did not report it.

I think that it's time that our great newspapers have at least the same objectivity, the same fullness of coverage, that television has. And I can only say thank God for television and radio for keeping the newspapers a little more honest.

Now, some newspapers don't fall in the category to which I have spoken, but I can only say that the great metropolitan newspapers in this field, they have a right to take every position they want on the editorial page, but on the news page they also have a right to have reporters cover men who have strong feelings whether they're for or against a candidate. But the responsibility also is to put a few Greenbergs on, on the candidate they happen to be against, whether they're against him on the editorial page or just philosophically deep down, a fellow who at least will report what the man says. . . .

I leave you gentlemen now and you will now write it. You will interpret it. That's your right. But as I leave you I want you to know—just think how much you're going to be missing.

You won't have Nixon to kick around any more, because, gentlemen, this is my last press conference and it will be one in which I have welcomed the opportunity to test wits with you. I have always respected you. I have sometimes disagreed with you.

But unlike some people, I've never canceled a subscription to a paper and also I never will.

I believe in reading what my opponents say and I hope that what I have said today will at least make television, radio and the press first recognize the great responsibility they have to report all the news and, second, recognize that they have a right and a responsibility, if they're against a candidate,

to give him the shaft, but also recognize if they give him the shaft, put one lonely reporter on the campaign who will report what the candidate says now and then.

Thank you, gentlemen, and good day.

The Comeback: 1968

Q. Mr. Nixon, you are finally living in the lap of luxury, you have it made—so why did you resume politics?

R.N. Whether I have it made or not has no reference to what I do. It gets back to my conviction that men at the highest level in politics do not choose their path. They can try all they want, but if it isn't the right time and the right place they're not going to get very far. In my case a series of events that nobody could have anticipated when I left California in 1963 has brought me back into politics. Those events were the terrible defeat of the Republican party in 1964, the emergence again of a grave foreign policy issue—the Vietnam war—and the feeling on the part of many Republicans that I could unite the party and that I could provide national leadership, particularly in foreign policy. I wouldn't say that these events created a draft, but they did create an attitude that made it inevitable that I would return to politics.

Once a man has been in politics, once that's been in his life, he will always return if the people want him. He cannot return unless they do. That's why I had no hesitancy about entering all the primaries. That decision was quite a risk at the time. All the polls showed Romney was going to win. But I felt that unless I could demonstrate that people wanted me the nomination would not mean anything.

Q. You have seen the Presidency in action. How would you operate as President?

R.N. For one thing, I would disperse power, spread it among able people. Men operate best only if they are given the chance to operate at full capacity.

I would operate differently from President Johnson. Instead of taking all power to myself, I'd select cabinet members who could do their jobs, and each of them would have the stature and the power to function effectively. Publicity would not center at the White House alone. Every key official would have the opportunity to be a big man in his field. On the other hand, when a President takes all the real power himself, those around him become puppets. They shrivel up and become less and less creative.

Actually, my belief in dispersal of power relates to the fundamental proposition of how to make a country move forward. Progress demands that you develop your most creative people to their fullest. And your most creative people can't develop in a monolithic, centralized power set-up.

Q. How would you label yourself?

R.N. Labels mean different things to different people. The nineteenth-century liberal is the twentieth-century conservative and the nineteenth-century conservative (with a small c) is the twentieth-century liberal. For example, in the conservative-liberal dialogue, which began in eighteenth-century America, probably the major difference was that the conservatives then were for strong central government. Hamilton was a strong central government man, whereas the liberals like Jefferson were for individual liberties, for decentralization of power.

In the twentieth century the liberals became the strong central government people —all power should be consolidated in Washington—and the conservatives became the people who were for decentralization.

Well, basically I'm a strong advocate of individual liberties. I'm very skeptical about centralized power. I believe in strong local government.

Now let's take this conservative-liberal dialogue as it relates to foreign policy. The conservatives have been considered the isolationists and the internationalists were considered to be the liberals. So looking at my record you would have to say I'm a liberal on foreign policy. Because I recognize America's role in the world I am not an isolationist. I have supported foreign aid, for instance.

But the old liberals who were internationalists 20 years ago now are turning inward. They are telling us to get out of Asia and Latin America, that we're overcommitted. My view, however, hasn't changed. While I make it very clear that we have to get other nations to assume their share of the responsibility, I also believe that we cannot withdraw from the world. Am I a conservative or a liberal? My answer is that I'm an internationalist.

By another foreign policy standard it is said that a conservative is basically anti-Communist and a liberal does not believe that Communism is a particular threat. By this test I've been called a conservative. But I don't see the Communist world as one world. I see the shades of gray. I see it as a multicolor thing. So rather than say I'm a conservative, I say I'm a firm opponent of totalitarianism of any kind and a strong proponent of freedom. If you want to describe me, you might say I'm a "whole-worlder." Too many people have been "half-worlders." Some have been able to see the danger in Asia but not in Europe and others have been able to see the danger in Europe but not in Asia. What we've got to see is the whole world.

On the race issue I'm a liberal. On economics I'm a conservative. Domestically, you could say I'm a centrist. But really I don't go for labels. You can't classify me. I'm a pragmatist, but not a pragmatist in the sense that I'm for anything merely because it works. I'm a pragmatist with some deep principles that never change. I'm just not doctrinaire. If there is one thing that classifies me it is that I'm a nonextremist.

23

Cesar Chavez

The name of Cesar Chavez has become synonymous with the farm workers movement in the 1970s. In fact, no other contemporary figure in the American labor movement has generated more controversy and publicity during the last decade than this disciplined advocate of non-violent protest.

In the tradition of Dr. Martin Luther King, Chavez has given to California's large Chicano population, and to migrant farm laborers, white and non-white, a sense of pride, unity and commitment to the elimination of social injustice and discrimination. The sympathetic selection that follows describes Chavez' early years as a migrant farm worker, his career as a labor organizer, and the implications of his success. It also gives some insight into the character of the man.

Ironically, the initial success of Chavez' UFWOC in the grape fields of Delano during the mid-1960s created a new problem for his cause: the emergence of a new and far more powerful rival for the farm worker's support, the Teamsters Union. Even so, the wide support that the Chavez grape boycott received from clergy, the press and other unions during the Delano strike raised at last the prospect of collective bargaining for all U.S. farm workers. How soon this will come is uncertain. And how important a part will Chavez and his union play when that day arrives?

The Chavez clan, headed by Cesar's grandparents, came to the United States as refugees from the Mexican revolution. Joining other displaced persons, they moved across the Southwest with the crops, but unlike most of the others, they were able to save enough to make a down payment on a farm of their own near the Colorado River in Arizona. There, in 1927, Cesar Estrada Chavez was born. His father's name, Librado, means Freedom.

The Chavez family managed to hold its land through most of the Depression, yielding only in 1938 to the combination of forces arrayed against small landowners. Migrants again, they started west, unprepared for the viciousness which California's farm labor jungle had assumed during the Depression.

For the next several years, they lived in their car, or in tents without heat or light; went without shoes in the winter; ate wild mustard greens to stay alive; were used mercilessly by labor contractors. In time, the family learned the tricks of labor contractors, learned where to find work, how long to stay, when to move on.

Like other migrant children, Cesar had to change schools several times each year, as his parents moved with the crops. The inadequacies of his education were compounded by the general substandardness of rural schools and by the traditional shunting of Spanish-speaking migrant children into segregated classrooms which provided little more than a child care service. Nevertheless, Chavez had completed the eighth grade by the time he was fourteen and had to leave school to work full-time in the fields.

In his early twenties, he married Helen Favila, daughter of a *zapatista* hero of the Mexican revolution. In 1949, the first of eight children was born to Cesar and Helen Chavez. Like most second-generation Mexican-Americans, they left the migrant stream, settling in San Jose, where Cesar worked in apricots and other local crops. During the off-season, he took whatever odd jobs he could find, such as lumber-stacking. In time, he would no doubt have left agricultural work altogether, but the farm labor movement changed his life—as he, in turn, was to change the farm labor movement.

The seed of farm worker organizing was planted early in Cesar Chavez. When he was about twelve, there was an insurgency within the Dried Fruit and Nut Packers Union of the AFL. Most of the members, including Cesar's father and uncle, wanted to affiliate with the CIO instead. During the controversy, young Cesar listened to their talk about the merits and demerits of various forms of unionism. Eventually, Warehousemen's Local No. 6 of the CIO won the dispute. Librado Chavez supported many other organizing efforts while his son watched and listened and learned.

Cesar and Helen Chavez lived on the east side of San Jose, on the "wrong side" of Highway 101. The area was known among its inhabitants, with representative Mexican humor, as Sal Si Puedes, which means "Get out if you can." At about this time, Father Donald McDonnell was building a mission in Sal Si Puedes, naming it after Our Lady of Guadalupe. The Virgin of Guadalupe, the "Dark Madonna," is an important unifying symbol among Mexicans, even those who are not practicing Catholics. This religious-national symbol was later to figure in Chavez's own organizing.

Night after night, Father McDonnell made the rounds of the barrio, talking with people about their problems, in their own homes. In due course, he knocked on Cesar

Chavez's door. It was perhaps the most important single meeting in the history of the farm labor movement. Then, in 1952, another crucial meeting took place: this one between Chavez and Fred Ross of the Community Service Organization.

The CSO was an outgrowth of the Industrial Areas Foundation, itself an outgrowth of Saul Alinsky's Back of the Yards movement which organized the lower-middle-class area around the Chicago stockyards in the early 1940's. The core of Alinsky's organizing philosophy is the belief that social change is more basic and lasting if the people affected by problems identify those problems for themselves and band together in interest-groups to deal with them. Alinsky enjoyed titillating friends and foes alike with frequent allusions to "radical" and "revolutionary," but his technique was actually a revolution against nothing so much as the paternalistic social-worker mentality.

In 1953, Cesar Chavez became a state-wide organizer for the CSO. He traveled to Oakland and southern Alameda County; up and down the San Joaquin Valley; to Oxnard, in Ventura County, where he transformed the Mexican-American colónia from a slack agglomeration of defeated men and women, displaced from the lemon groves by braceros, into a tautly mobilized group which won the jobs back through collective action.

Chavez's organizing skills were so evident that, in 1960, he was appointed General Director of the national CSO. With the help, among others, of Dolores Huerta, who became his principal assistant, he built the CSO to a strength of twenty-two active chapters in California and Arizona.

As a direct result of CSO efforts, two major pieces of legislation were enacted. Old Age Security benefits were extended to first-generation Mexicans even if they had not become naturalized citizens; and the state disability insurance program was extended to agricultural workers.

When the 1962 CSO convention failed to adopt an all-out farm labor program, Chavez submitted his resignation. He had devoted ten years to the CSO, and he did not make this decision lightly.

With no outside support of any kind, Chavez began in 1962 to organize agricultural workers. In order to avoid any suggestion that the organization would function immediately as an orthodox trade union, he called it the Farm Workers Association.

Chavez knew that the stereotype of farm workers' homogeneity was false. He knew that Mexican, Anglo, Filipino, and Negro agricultural laborers were often suspicious of one another. He knew that the concerns of out-of-state migrants were not quite the same as the concerns of in-state migrants, and that neither were the same as the interests of the home guard. He knew that many farm workers were likely, at first, to be apathetic or even antagonistic toward unionization: year-round hands who thought of themselves as part of management; green carders who wanted only to return to Mexico with as much money and little trouble as possible; wetbacks who were subject to deportation if they attracted any attention; wounded, disillusioned veterans of previous organizing drives which had failed; housewives, students, and other casual workers who had no intention of remaining in agriculture.

Every night, fighting his fatigue after working in the fields all day, Chavez went to the homes of this type of worker, explaining the Farm Workers Association, pointing out the short-run kinds of things members could do by working together: they could form a credit union; help one another with workmen's compensation and other quasi-legal problems; get preferential rates on insurance.

By the middle of 1964, the Association was self-supporting. It had perhaps a thousand dues-paying members, in more than fifty local groups, spread over seven counties. Chavez no longer needed to work in the fields. The primary problem now became one of satisfying the members' desire for accomplishment, without entering into precipitate adventures of the type which had led to the demise of so many earlier farm labor organizations.

FWA took a "militant" position for the first time in May, 1965, when it assisted a rent strike against the Tulare County Housing Authority, to protest rent increases of 40 percent at two farm labor camps with very substandard facilities. In the summer of 1965, there were two small strikes, involving FWA members on horticultural farms. Both won their objectives: wage increases, and the rehiring of members who had been discharged.

No matter how sound its basic plan, how shrewd its day-to-day tactics, and how great the magnetism of its leaders, the career of every social movement is shaped at many crucial points by historical accidents and by unbelievers who know not what they do. The "Delano movement"—which, after September, 1965, the FWA was often called —began fortuitously, and at critical junctures received help from unlikely sources.

When Public Law 78 ended on December 31, 1964, the U.S. Department of Labor continued to admit braceros to California simply by calling them something else and changing the rules slightly. The 1965 rules required payment of $1.40 an hour. Through this requirement, quite unintentionally, the Department of Labor, never renowned as a fearless friend of the farm labor movement, helped set the stage for events in Delano.

The second major impetus came from the self-organized Filipino workers who had joined *AWOC* six years earlier, and were never members of FWA at all. The AWOC representative assigned to this Filipino group was Larry Itliong. In 1929, when he was fifteen, Itliong had left his home in the Philippines to come to the United States. He had worked in the fields for some years,

then moved into the Northwest fishing and canning industries where he helped organize his compatriots. When he joined the staff of AWOC, he made his headquarters in Delano, which served as "home base" for a sizable number of Filipino agricultural workers.

Table grapes are among the crops in which Filipinos have long specialized. California grapes ripen first in the Coachella Valley each year. There, in May, 1965, fortuitous links began coming together into the start of a long chain.

Coachella Valley growers were told by the Department of Labor that they would have to pay braceros $1.40 an hour. Filipino grape pickers felt they were entitled to the same rate. When they did not receive it, they turned for help to Larry Itliong and AWOC. There was a brief work stoppage. Largely through the leverage of the growers' desire for braceros, the Filipinos won their wage demand.

By September, many of these same workers had moved north to the Delano area, where the table grape season was just beginning. The growers were offering $1.20 an hour, plus a "bonus" of five cents per man per box. The workers saw no reason why they should get less than they had in the Coachella Valley. A majority—some say as many as 90 percent—of the Filipinos walked off their jobs.

From the beginning of the strike on September 8, it was taken for granted that FWA members would not cross the Filipinos' picket lines into the premises of the ten struck grower-shippers. But would they be strikebreaking if they continued picking other grapes in the Delano area? It was a painful dilemma for Chavez and the other FWA leaders. They calculated they were about two years away from being prepared for a major strike. On the other hand, how could they permit themselves to give the appearance of scabbing on another farm workers' organization? They decided to put the question to a vote of the FWA membership.

An emergency meeting was called for September 16, the 145th anniversary of the independence of Mexico from Spain. The largest hall in Delano overflowed, with many members standing outside. Emotions were overflowing, too. When no one voiced any misgivings about extending the strike to all Delano grape growers, Chavez took it upon himself to explain how great the sacrifices would be and how limited were FWA's resources.

Nonetheless, the vote for *la huelga* (the strike) was unanimous.

Veteran labor reporters for California's metropolitan newspapers said the strike could not possibly be won. Since collective bargaining laws did not apply to agriculture, it was a naked test of strength, and how could the strength of penniless farm workers compare with that of multimillion-dollar corporations?

Paying no attention to the labor experts, Chavez and the other members of the FWA executive committee invented their own precedents as they went along. They decided to follow the grapes out of the fields and to try to upset the distribution system. Some individual members of the Teamsters respected the FWA picket lines. Members of the International Longshoremen's and Warehousemen's Union refused to load "hot" grapes.

On December 18, 1965, a few days after the boycott began, Walter Reuther came to Delano. He pledged $5,000 a month support from his United Automobile Workers union. Reuther had never visited AWOC, in Stockton, when it might have used his leadership between 1959 and 1962. He evidently sensed that the Delano movement had far different prospects from those of the old AWOC.

In March, 1966, Senator Harrison Williams, Democrat of New Jersey, brought his Subcommittee on Migratory Labor to California for public hearings.

On the final day of the hearings, Senator Robert F. Kennedy lent his full influence to the FWA cause.

From this public relations triumph, FWA vaulted immediately to another, a march to the state capitol in Sacramento to petition Governor Pat Brown to do something about collective bargaining rights for farm workers.

The length of the march was more than 230 miles: nearly the same, coincidentally, as Gandhi's Salt March to the sea in 1933. For twenty-five days, the Delano pilgrims marched.

On April 6, just four days before Easter, the line of march was galvanized by news which seemed heaven-sent: Schenley had agreed to recognize FWA and to negotiate a contract covering all Schenley field workers in the Delano area. The boycott had won its objective. On the following day, an even more astounding development was announced. After years of implacable opposition to farm unions, officials of the Di Giorgio Corporation suddenly announced that they were offering representation elections.

The company then played its trump card, announcing that the Teamsters union would make a good representative for its Delano workers, and should be included on the ballot. The Teamsters graciously agreed.

The Teamster campaign was conducted by professionals who did not scruple to use such tactics as red-baiting and race-baiting.

On August 22, FWA and AWOC merged into a new entity, known as the United Farm Workers Organizing Committee (UFWOC), AFL-CIO. Cesar Chavez became director; Larry Itliong, assistant director.

The official results were announced on September 2. UFWOC had received 530 votes, the Teamsters, 331; 12 workers preferred no union. Cesar Chavez and his dedicated band of amateurs had won a contest against the largest, richest union in the world in league with one of the largest agricultural corporations.

To this point, UFWOC had undertaken three major boycotts; all had ended in contracts. To Chavez and other UFWOC strategists, it seemed clear that the consumer boycott was the most viable answer, perhaps the only answer, to the singular problems of farm labor organizing: What do you do when you represent a majority of workers and employers still refuse to acknowledge your existence?

Mayors or city councils of Cleveland, Detroit, San Francisco, and other cities endorsed the table-grape boycott. So did the legislature of the entire State of Hawaii. New York City was nearly completely "shut down."

All the contenders for the 1968 Democratic presidential nomination supported farm workers' right to collective bargaining, and supported the boycott as a legitimate device to secure that right. Hubert Humphrey, after he won the nomination, met personally with Cesar Chavez.

The boycott has been astonishingly effective, both in terms of public education and in its impact on grape sales.

Old suspicions, jealousies, and feelings of superiority or inferiority have begun to fade between Anglos, Mexicans, Filipinos, and Negroes, as they work together in the Delano movement. The old feelings have not entirely disappeared. Some of the Filipinos who gave so much to the movement feel that they have been slighted in the UFWOC structure, and that their representation on the executive committee—Larry Itliong and Philip Vera Cruz—is "tokenism." Some Anglo fruit pickers from Oklahoma and Arkansas consider UFWOC a "Meskin" union, and want no part of it. Some Mexicans and Filipinos want to keep Anglos out because they are afraid of being "taken over."

If any criticism were justified, it would be that Chavez has leaned overly heavily on Anglo aides who are not and never have been farm workers.

This was a major departure from Chavez's original ideal of farm workers' self-sufficiency. But when FWA was thrust into the grape strike with only a few days' notice, survival required instant expertise in economic research, law, fund-raising, writing, and other technical skills which farm workers did not possess. UFWOC owes its existence to Anglos who volunteered such skills, as well as to the strikers who provided the "infantry."

It is doubtful that Cesar Chavez ever imagined he would become a symbol for "brown consciousness"—for *la raza* (all persons of Mexican ancestry, whether first, second, third generation or more)—but that is what he has become.

During the early years of FWA, the Spanish-speaking organizations ignored Chavez—and he tried to ignore them.

But by the time of the peregrinación to Sacramento in the spring of 1966, it was apparent to even the most jaundiced observers that Chavez was without selfish ambitions.

Old rivalries began to drop away.

By surviving—in the face of great adversity, Chavez and the United Farm Workers Organizing Committee have had a substantial impact on the American labor movement.

Organized labor has given UFWOC at least $600,000 since 1965. It has given perhaps as much again in legal and technical counsel, contributions in kind, lobbying assistance.

One of the problems with which a successful social movement must deal is the problem of success itself. In some ways, Cesar Chavez probably wishes that he and his movement were not so widely known. With coverage in *Time, The New Yorker,* and many other national publications, has come a mounting number of requests for help from farm workers in other areas.

At one time, Chavez felt there could be no harm in lending the UFWOC name to self-starting efforts in Florida, Wisconsin, Texas, and elsewhere. But he soon learned otherwise. Debts were incurred; political allies were confused; and, most serious, local farm workers' hopes were raised in vain.

From then on, Chavez firmly rejected distractions and dilutions of effort.

The Delano movement has introduced a number of innovative techniques which have not been lost on social reformers engaged in other movements.

One of the earliest Delano innovations was a newspaper, entitled *El Malcriado,* unlike any other labor paper published in this country.

From its first issue, *El Malcriado* was a saucy, free-swinging affair, in which news and editorials were often indistinguishable, and generously spiced with cartoons, invective, and jokes, sometimes verging on the slanderous.

Of all Chavez's innovations, the most fundamental is his attempt to build a union which is not just a vending machine—not like the unions which increasingly resemble the businesses they meet across the bargaining table.

A cooperative gas station is already in operation. There is a clinic. Chavez's first attempt at a community institution, the credit union, is still functioning.

How "radical" is Cesar Chavez? Tremendously. Not very. Everything depends on one's point of view, and one's terms.

If "radical" means "getting to the root," if it means facing realities unflinchingly and without cant, then Chavez is a genuine radical.

A successful farm labor union will by its very nature "subvert" the present rural California social order under which elected representatives and administrators have served the minority who own the land rather than the majority who work on it.

But in the usual, pejorative sense of the word, Chavez, and farm workers generally, are not "radical" at all. Farm laborers believe in the American dream.

The desires of farm workers are essentially conservative, in that they include only those things which the American economy has demonstrated it is quite capable of conferring upon other workers: reasonable wages, reasonable safety and other working conditions, reasonable fringe benefits, reasonable job security, and underlying all a reasonable voice in determining what is reasonable. The present-day California farm labor movement does not call for the breaking up of great estates and redistribution of the land.

Despite many disappointments, Chavez, other UFWOC leaders, and the membership retain a basic confidence in the democratic process.

The Delano movement benefited from America's discovery of poverty in the early 1960's, from the *aggiornamento,* or refreshing, of Catholicism under Pope John XXIII, from the civil rights movement, the student movement, the peace movement, and, most recently, from the ecology movement.

But ripe times do not, by themselves, make movements, much less sustain them through the crises and countermovements which any effective social movement is bound to generate. One keeps coming back, again and again, to Cesar Chavez.

How to account for it? Everything about the man is low-key. He is slightly below the middle height. His handshake is diffident. His smile is shy. He issues no crisp orders, but says, "What would you think if we tried such-and-such?"

He enters a public meeting so unobstrusively that one is hardly aware of his presence until he is introduced to speak. He never raises his voice in public utterances, any more than private.

Of all the ways Cesar Chavez has changed the content of men's lives, none is more fundamental, none more daring, and none will be remembered longer than the covenant with nonviolence which he himself has made, and which he asks all UFWOC members to make.

One of the qualities which Chavez brings to his leadership—which others did not—is that he is nothing but a farm laborer and farm labor organizer. He has no other profession to fall back on, as the others did. He will stay with the job until it is finished, or until it finishes him.

In the traditional culture of Mexico, women's place is in *las casa*.

Cesar Chavez has been a liberator in this respect. When the strike began, Dolores Huerta was made director of picketing. No one was more successful than she in persuading workers to leave the vineyards. Other women began to grow more vocal and to assume positions outside the strike kitchen.

The UFWOC discipline apparently did not forbid verbal violence, and there seems to have been a good deal of it. And sometimes the ban on physical violence wavered. A few pickets peppered strikebreakers with marbles. A few growers' tires were flattened. A few windows in strikebreakers' homes were broken. But, by and large, the discipline was well maintained—astonishingly well maintained under the particular circumstances.

Chavez is challenging the long-standing, deeply embedded folkways which equate aggressiveness with manliness in the cultures of Mexico, the Philippines, the United States—and in the culture of labor organizing itself.

Since the death of Martin Luther King, Chavez is probably America's leading practitioner of nonviolent direct action in the resolution of social problems where channels of communication and mediation are blocked or do not exist. Indeed, he is one of the great nonviolent reformers of the world. Some observers anticipate that if he continues to develop his ideas about social change, and applies them as he has done to date, Chavez will in time be considered for the Nobel Peace Prize.

Others anticipate that Cesar Chavez himself may be martyred, like his friends Kennedy and King. If the thought has crossed his mind, he does not speak of it, and it does not affect him in the slightest. He seems fully prepared to accept whatever may come his way.